The Breadfruit Cookbook

The Ulu Cookbook

www.ulucookbook.com

Fae Hirayama

For additional copies contact: Handworks
                                   P.O. Box 215
                                   Kapaa, Hawaii 96746

Foreword

The breadfruit, or ulu is this cook's delight. In its green, immature state, it works in all my recipes that call for artichoke heart. When still green but mature, it is my potato, taro and sometimes rice substitute. When ripe, I use it in place of sweet potato, yam, pumpkin, chestnut and banana. But the ripe, roasted ulu filled with butter and brown sugar will always be my sentimental favorite because this is the way my grandmother introduced ulu to me. In her way, whenever there was something new to be had, she would say to me, "you wait 'til pau cook, ono." It was always true. Whatever she cooked, was wonderfully good.

When I moved into my house on family land, I asked my father to help me plant a breadfruit tree in my yard. It was a third generation plant by way of my uncle. My father asked me what I was going to do with all the breadfruit. I planned to eat some and to give some away. The first year the breadfruit fruited, I was able to keep up with giving away the fruits on my small tree by taking it to friends, to the food bank and to any one else who was interested. By the second year, the tree had more than doubled in size and I had more than I needed or could give away. So began the annual Ulu dinners.

On the eve of the 5th Annual Ulu Dinner, while the ulu tree is bearing flowers and fruit once more, the collection of what has become known as the ulu recipes is now a book. Our dinners have become the Ulu Festival with the few claiming attendance to all dinners as "charter members".

The ulu pastelles have become the annual favorite served with traditional meat filling and with a vegetarian filling.

This book embodies the spirit of joining together and the years of sharing our stories of the best, ulu we ever had including Roasted Ulu, and ulu packed tight in the pot cooked with coconut milk until sticky, ulu custard pie and ulu ice cream. Comfort food at its finest. For those who enjoy a lighter fare, Marinated Ulu "Artichoke," Ulu "Artichoke" Pesto and Ulu Pasta Salad are favorites.

Visit us at:

www.ulucookbook.com

Table of Contents

FOREWORD

CHAPTER 1: Traditional
1   Baked Ripe Ulu with Butter and Brown Sugar
2   Baked Ulu with Coconut milk
3   Fire Roasted Ulu
4   Fire Roasted Ulu with Corned Beef
5   Fried Ulu
5   Portuguese Style Boiled Ulu
6   Tahitian Roasted Ulu with Corned Beef
7   Ulu Poi
7   Baked Ulu Pudding
8   Ulu with Coconut Milk
8   Ulu with Codfish and Onion

CHAPTER 2: Immature Green Ulu "Artichoke"
9   Hot Ulu "Artichoke" Dip
10   Italian Stuffed Ulu "Artichoke"
12   Marinated Ulu "Artichoke"
13   Tomato and Ulu "Artichoke" Salad
14   Ulu "Artichoke" and Chicken Pasta Salad
15   Ulu "Artichoke" and Shrimp Salad
16   Ulu "Artichoke" Appetizer
17   Ulu "Artichoke" Bruchetta
18   Ulu "Artichoke" Curry "Rice" Salad
19   Ulu "Artichoke" Frittata
20   Ulu "Artichoke" Pasta Pesto Salad
21   Ulu "Artichoke" Pesto
22   Ulu "Artichoke" with Garlic

CHAPTER 2: Mature Ulu – Side Dish
23   Candied Ulu
24   Chirashi Ulu
25   Crispy Ulu Baskets
26   Garlic Mashed Ulu
27   Grilled Ulu Chips

CHAPTER 3: Side Dishes – *continued*

28 Mashed Ulu
29 Mazemeshi Ulu
30 Mushrooms Stuffed with Garlic Mashed Ulu
31 Portuguese Style Twice Cooked Ulu
32 Roasted Ulu with Garlic
33 Roasted Ulu with Olives
34 Scalloped Ulu
35 Scalloped Ulu with Cheese
36 Shoyu Sugar Ulu
36 Sweet Ulu Chips
37 Ulu and Shrimp Tempura
38 Ulu Chips
39 Ulu Dinner Fries
40 Ulu Hash Browns
41 Ulu Inarizushi
42 Ulu Shoe String Potatoes
43 Ulu Stuffing
44 Ulu with Cheese Stuffed Mushrooms

CHAPTER 4: Mature Ulu – Breads and Noodles

45 Plain Ulu Biscuits
46 Ulu Kugel
47 Ulu Latke
48 Ulu Lavosh
49 Ulu Noodles
50 Ulu Pancakes
51 Ulu Pierogies
55 Ulu Quick Bread
56 Sweet Ulu Biscuits

CHAPTER 5 Mature Ulu – Soups and Salads

55 Codfish and Ulu Salad
56 Creamy Ulu and Kale Soup
57 Hot German Style Ulu Salad
58 Hot Seafood Salad

CHAPTER 5: Soups and Salads – *continued*

59   Ulu Noodle Soup
60   Ulu "Potato" Salad
61   Ulu Clam Chowder
63   Ulu Corn Chowder
64   Ulu Vegan Vegetable Soup
65   Ulu Vegetable Soup
66   Ulu with Sun Dried Tomatoes and Capers

CHAPTER 6: Mature Ulu – Main Dishes

67   Baked Stuffed Ulu
68   Chicken Adobo with Ulu
68   Chinese Style Ulu Cakes
69   Kimchee Fried Rice Style Ulu
70   New England Style Boiled Dinner with Ulu
71   Portuguese Style Boiled Dinner with Ulu
72   Pot Roast Chicken with Ulu
73   Salmon Croquettes
74   Savory Chili Stuffed Ulu
75   Ulu and Ham Casserole
76   Ulu Chicken Curry
77   Ulu Codfish Patties
78   Ulu Corned Beef Hash
79   Ulu Crusted Fish
80   Ulu Frittata
81   Ulu Pastelles
82   Ulu Corned Beef Hash Patties
83   Ulu Pot Pastelles
84   Ulu Pot Pie
85   Ulu Shepard's Pie
86   Ulu Spinach Lasagna
88   Ulu Stuffed with Pork Hash
89   Ulu Tuna Patties
90   Ulu with Pigeon Peas
91   Vegetable Ulu Curry
92   Vegetarian Ulu Lasagna
94   Vegetarian Ulu Nishime
96   Vegetarian Ulu Pastelles

CHAPTER 6: Ripe Ulu – Desserts

97   Baked Ulu Mochi with Coconut
98   Crispy Sweet Ulu Balls
98   Halo Halo with Sweet Ulu
99   Layered Ulu Manju
100 Stuffed Sweet Ulu
100 Sweet Ulu Andagi
101 Sweet Ulu Chien Doi
102 Sweet Ulu Crunch
103 Sweet Ulu Fritters
104 Sweet Ulu Ice Cream
105 Sweet Ulu Lavosh
106 Sweet Ulu Lumpia
106 Sweet Ulu Macadamia Nut Bread
107 Sweet Ulu Manju
108 Sweet Ulu Mochi
108 Sweet Ulu Mochi with Kinako
109 Sweet Ulu Won Ton with Honey
110 Ulu "Sweet Potato" Pie
111 Ulu Coffee Cake
112 Custard Pie
113 Ulu Dorayaki
114 Ulu Ice Cake
115 Ulu Yokan

Notes
  Substitutions

Chapter 1

Traditional

Traditional Breadfruit, ulu, recipes use the mature breadfruit. An "*Ulu Story*" accompanies many of the recipes in this section. These are "old fashioned", home style recipes that are traditionally associated with breadfruit.

Baked Ulu with Butter and Brown sugar
My sentimental favorite

Ulu Story: My grandmother loved to eat ulu. For years, I thought Ulu had to be cooked in the ashes of a fire...wrapped in foil so that the edges burned just a little and the insides were chewy and brown. She would pull out the core and trim out the edge just a bit then cut a block of butter in half and push it into the center of the ulu. She then followed it with a spoonful of brown sugar careful to cover the top with foil. She would take the ulu outside and bury it in the ashes. Nothing smelled as good as the ulu as it cooked. When the ulu was done, she cut it into quarters, and we ate it scraping the wonderful sweet, sticky brown bits near the skin!

1 ripe ulu
¼ cup or ½ block butter
3 tablespoons brown sugar

Wash a ripe ulu. Pull out the stem and core. Trim top edge of ulu if needed. Fill cavity with butter and brown sugar. Cover ulu with foil and place in a baking pan with 1cup water. Bake for 1 hour at 350 degrees.

To serve, unwrap ulu and cut in half lengthwise. Bring to the table on a shallow bowl with a large spoon. Scoop to serve, making sure each piece is topped with the sugar and butter syrup from the center of the ulu.

Baked Ulu with Coconut Milk
A baked variation of a South Pacific favorite

1 half ripe or mature, green ulu
1 12 ounce can frozen Coconut milk
1 cup water

Wash, core and peel ulu. Cut into 1½ inch chunks. Place ulu in a baking pan, cover with coconut milk and water. Cover pan with foil. Bake for 1 hour at 325 degrees.

Fire Roasted Ulu
A traditional Island Favorite

Ulu Story: I brought some Ulu pastelles to a friend's nail salon and the conversation turned to the upcoming Ulu Fest. He just finished "waxing nostalgic" about Ulu Crusted Salmon with Dill when the woman at the next station told us a story about how her father would roast Ulu on the fire and burn the skin...Her eyes lit up and she told us of how the skin had to be charred and how it would crack when her father would finally open the blackened Ulu. The inside was soft and a little sweet with the roasted flavor all the way through, but the best part was the browned edges, next to the skin.

1 Ulu, half ripe

Pierce ulu deeply in 3 or 4 places. Roast a mature ulu (firm outside, slightly soft inside) over charcoal, in hot ashes or directly over a gas burner. Turn the fruit as it begins to char. Roasting takes about 60 minutes. When the stem end of the ulu starts to steam, ulu is cooked. Remove ulu from fire. Cut out stem and core. Scoop out cooked ulu or peel off charred outer skin and cut into slices to serve.

Alternative: This oven method is useful when preparing Ulu for a large group of people. Pierce ulu. Place Ulu in oven under broiler. Turn ulu to brown all sided. When skin is evenly brown, turn off broiler, and bake in oven at 350 degrees for about 1 hour.

Fire Roasted Ulu with Corned Beef
A traditional Tahitian favorite

Ulu Story: *A friend told me that he had the best ulu he ever ate while visiting Tahiti. The ulu was fire roasted, burned on the outside and filled with corned beef. When the ulu was cooked, the stem and core were removed. The center was filled with corned beef and the ulu was "plugged up" and returned to the fire.*

1 mature Ulu
1 can corned beef

Pierce ulu deeply in 3 or 4 places. Roast a firm mature ulu over charcoal or directly over a gas burner. Turn the fruit as it begins to char. Roast about 60 minutes. When the stem end of the ulu starts to steam, ulu is cooked.

Remove ulu from fire. Cut out stem and core careful to keep the stem end intact. Fill cavity with canned corned beef. Close cavity with ulu stem and return to fire until fruit starts steaming. Cut open and scoop out cooked ulu along with the hot corned beef.

Fried Ulu

1 large mature ulu, peeled and cored
2 cloves garlic
1 chili pepper
4 tablespoons butter
salt to taste

Cut ulu into quarters. Boil ulu until tender, covered with water with garlic and chili pepper until tender.

Slice ulu in ½ to ¾ inch thick wedges. Fry until light brown in butter. Add more butter as needed while cooking successive batches. Serve hot.

Optional: Fry ulu in 2 tablespoons butter and
            2 tablespoons olive oil.

Portuguese Style Boiled Ulu

1 large mature ulu, peeled, cored
2 cloves garlic
1 chili pepper
1 tablespoon salt

Cut Ulu into wedges. Boil ulu covered with water with garlic and chili pepper until tender.

Tahitian Roasted Ulu with Corned Beef
A Tahitian Favorite

Ulu Story: I bought a 16 foot long, extending painters pole at our local paint store to use as my Ulu picker. While I was there, I told the man who helped me that I was going to make an Ulu picker and told me his family's favorite way to cook Ulu. They would pick a mature ulu, one that was turning brown on the outside but still feels hard and has milky sap at the stem when picked. The ulu was cooked Tahitian style, roasted over a fire. After the ulu was roasted, it was scooped out and cooked with browned, canned corned beef, the one with the orange label from New Zealand, and a little onion (add 2 cans if "got plenty guys"). Fresh coconut milk was poured on just before serving.

1 Roasted Ulu (grilled or in ashes)
1 can, 12 ounces corned beef
1 medium onion
12 ounces coconut milk

Roast ulu until soft and scoop out pulp. In a large heavy bottom pan, cook corned beef and onions until browned, adding roasted ulu. Just before serving, top with fresh coconut milk and serve when just heated through. Do not boil coconut milk as it will curdle.

Ulu Poi

1 large mature green or half ripe ulu

Peel, core and cut ulu into 1-2 inch wedges. Boil until soft. Remove ulu, reserving cooking water. Mash while still warm until it forms a thick paste. Add small amounts of reserved cooking water to "thin" ulu to desired consistency. Eat fresh, refrigerate unused portion.

The Hawaiians made ulu into poi when taro was unavailable. This poi was considered inferior but I find it a tasty alternative especially when half ripe ulu is used.

Ulu Pudding

1 ripe ulu
1 12 ounce can frozen Coconut milk
½ cup sugar

Mix ulu pulp coconut milk and sugar. Pour into a baking pan coated with cooking spray. Bake at 350 degrees until pudding is set (about 1 hour).

Ulu with Coconut Milk

1 Mature green or half ripe ulu
1 12 ounce can frozen coconut milk
2 cups water

Wash peel and core ulu. Cut into wedges and pack into a dutch oven or pot with cover. Cover ulu with water and coconut milk. Cook on low heat until ulu is tender and all the liquids are absorbed.

Ulu with Codfish and Onion

1 large mature ulu, peeled, cored
4 ounces dried codfish, shredded
½ cup sliced onion
¼ cup oil
salt to taste

Cut ulu into ¾ inch wedges. Boil ulu covered with water. Drain ulu. Toss with shredded codfish, sliced onion and oil.

Substitute: Chunk tuna and Shoyu to taste for codfish.

Chapter 2

Immature Green Breadfruit
Ulu "Artichoke"

 Immature green breadfruit, ulu, once cooked, has a taste and texture like an artichoke heart. The entire ulu can be eaten, as the core is tender. When using larger immature ulu, the core may become tough and can be trimmed after it is cooked. The skin of the immature ulu is very bumpy and the fruit is bright green. Pick the ulu when it is about 3-4 inches in diameter, about tennis ball sized. When picked, the stem of the immature ulu drips with white milky sap. To avoid getting the sticky latex stuck on the skin, immediately soak the ulu in water for 10-15 minutes. Be sure to rinse the container when the ulu is removed to prevent the sap from sticking on the bottom. Remove any of the white sap from the skin as soon as possible or it will stick to the skin even after it is cooked. Trim off any bits of sap with a paring knife.

Boiled Immature Ulu "Artichoke"

Boil the immature green Ulu whole. It takes about 60 minutes of cooking before it is tender. Using a pressure cooker (quick cool method) reduces cooking time to about 20 minutes, 15 minutes at high pressure and 5 to 10 minutes of conventional boiling. Be sure to follow your pressure cooker directions carefully.

Hot Ulu "Artichoke" Dip
A variation of a classic "hot" dip

1 cup marinated ulu "artichokes" (See
   recipe on page 12)
½ package frozen spinach, thawed and squeezed
2 cups sour cream (or substitute 2 tablespoons
   vinegar plus soy or dairy milk to make 2 cups)
½ medium onion cut into chunks
½ cup grated Parmesan cheese (or soy cheese)
2 teaspoons fresh basil or thyme, chopped
2 eggs

In a large food processor bowl with chopping blade, pulse until coarsely chopped, marinate ulu artichokes, spinach and onion. Add remaining ingredients and pulse until mixed but vegetables still chunky. Pour into a 1- quart sized baking dish. Bake at 325 degrees for 40-50 minutes until brown a bubbly. Serve with crackers or sliced vegetables.

This is a great way to use leftover marinated "artichokes"

Italian Stuffed "Artichoke"

2 green immature ulu

Stuffing:
          1 loaf fresh bread wheat or white bread
             (tear into ¾ inch pieces, about 4 cups)
          1 tablespoon light olive oil
          1 medium onion, (1 cup) chopped fine
          2 pieces Italian sausage, skin removed
          1 stalk celery chopped fine
          2 cloves garlic minced or crushed
          1 cup fresh mushrooms chopped
          ¼ cup Italian flat leaf parsley chopped
          1 tablespoon fresh basil and thyme
          ½ tablespoon fresh rosemary
          1 cup water or chicken stock
          ½ teaspoon salt (to taste)
          ½ teaspoon ground black pepper

Boil ulu whole in water, about 60 minutes or until tender (pierce with fork or chopstick). Place in a bowl of water to cool. (May be cooked ahead and kept in the refrigerator). Cut each ulu in half and scoop out core. Set aside.

Tear bread into ¾ inch pieces . Spread in a single layer on a cookie sheet and allow to dry. In a large pot, heat oil, add onions, celery and garlic. Cook until transparent with minimal browning. Add Italian sausage, skin removed and broken into pieces. Cook until brown.

Drain excess oil after browning sausage. Add mushrooms and cook for 2-3 minutes then adding

Italian Stuffed "Artichoke" - *continued*

chicken stock or water herbs, salt, pepper and simmer for 2-3 minutes more. Add bread pieces and stir well to combine. Reduce heat and cook until heated through.

Fill breadfruit halves with stuffing, mounding generously. Place stuffed ulu in a baking dish (spray with cooking spray or lightly oil pan). Bake in a 350 degree oven 30-45 minutes until tops are brown.

Marinated Ulu "Artichokes"
Artichokes of the Pacific

2 immature, green ulu
¼ round onion, sliced thin

Dressing:
  1/3 cup olive oil
  1/3 cup balsamic or white vinegar
  1 clove garlic crushed
  1 tablespoon fresh basil, sliced thin
  (or any combination of thyme, oregano or rosemary)
  1/2 teaspoon salt
  1/4 teaspoon fresh ground pepper
  2 tablespoons lemon juice or orange juice
    (optional)

Boil whole immature ulu until fork tender, about 1 hour. Chill until cold or plunge in ice water until cold. Slice into wedges or chunks as desired. Toss with dressing above and serve with onion garnish.

Tomato and Ulu "Artichoke" Salad

1 green immature Ulu, sliced
1 large beefsteak or 4 to 5 Roma tomatoes sliced
1 sweet onion sliced very thin.
Whole fresh basil leaves
Whole fresh oregano leaves

Dressing: ½ cup olive oil
            ¼ cup balsamic or red wine vinegar
            1 clove garlic cut

Rub cut side of garlic on platter. Arrange ulu slices, onion and tomato slices or thin wedges on a large platter. Top with whole basil and oregano leaves or alternate a basil and oregano leaf between tomato and ulu "pair". Pour dressing over slices or serve with oil and red vinegar on the "side".

Alternative: Toss everything gently in a bowl. Serve in butter lettuce leaf cups.

Ulu "Artichoke" and Chicken Pasta Salad

2 large chicken breasts, skin removed
Marinade: ¼ cup ulu pesto (recipe on page 21)
              2 tablespoons balsamic vinegar
              1 teaspoon soy sauce

2 cooked immature green ulu
Marinade: 2 cloves garlic crushed
              ¼ cup white or rice vinegar
              ¼ cup light olive oil
              ¼ cup chopped white onion
              2 tablespoon fresh basil, chopped

12 ounces pasta, boiled until firm in salted water
½ cup ulu pesto
¼ cup whole pine nuts
½ teaspoon salt
¼ teaspoon black pepper

Quarter and slice immature ulu into ¼ inch thick pieces and add to marinade, set aside.

Marinate Chicken breast in ¼ cup ulu pesto, soy sauce and balsamic vinegar. Grill for 10 minutes on each side until done. Set aside to cool; cut into ¾ inch cubes. Mix with ½ cup ulu pesto when cool. Add marinated ulu, pasta, pine nuts and season with salt and pepper. Chill thoroughly before serving.

Ulu "Artichoke" and Shrimp Salad
"Artichokes" of the Pacific

2 immature, green ulu
¼ round onion, sliced thin
12 ounces frozen, cooked shelled shrimp

Dressing:
     1/3 cup olive oil
     1/3 cup balsamic or white vinegar
     1 clove garlic crushed
     1 tablespoon fresh basil, sliced thin
        (or any combination of thyme, oregano
        or rosemary)
     ½ teaspoon salt
     ¼ teaspoon fresh ground pepper
     2 tablespoons lemon juice or orange juice
     (optional)

Boil whole immature ulu until fork tender, about 1 hour. Chill until cold or plunge in ice water. Slice into wedges or chunks as desired.

Toss sliced ulu and frozen shrimp with dressing above and serve with round onion garnish.

This is a great buffet dish!

Ulu "Artichoke" Appetizer

2 immature, green ulu

Dip:

 ½ cup mayonnaise (or Veganaise tm)
 2 tablespoons lemon juice
 1 clove crushed garlic
 ½ teaspoon salt
 ¼ teaspoon fresh ground black pepper
 2 to 3 drops hot sauce (optional)

Boil whole immature ulu until fork tender, about 1 hour. Chill until cold or plunge in ice water to chill. Slice ulu in half lengthwise then into ¼ inch thick slices. Serve arranged on a platter with Dip.

Ulu "Artichoke" Bruschetta
A variation of a French classic

2 immature green ulu, boiled
2 cloves garlic sliced
olive oil
Sliced basil leaves
*Parmesan or mozzarella cheese optional

2 12- inch sweet French baguettes (not sour
    dough)
olive oil
4 garlic cloves
Balsamic vinegar and olive oil

Boil immature green ulu until tender.   Slice lengthwise into quarters then ¼ inch slices. Cook gently in olive oil and garlic. Set aside to cool

Slice bread on a diagonal 3/8 to 1/2 inch thick. Toast under broiler for 1 minute until there is a very light crust.   Rub one side with cut side of garlic and brush both sides with olive oil. Return toast to broiler for 1 to 2 minutes on each side until golden brown and crunchy or bake at 400 degrees for 10 minutes.

Place sliced ulu on top of toasted bread. Top with a curl of cheese and thin slivers of sweet basil or tiny, whole, fresh basil leafs.   (Cuban basil is great)

Arrange on a large platter. Drizzle with balsamic vinegar and olive oil before serving.

Ulu "Artichoke" Curry Rice Salad

3 cups cooked white or brown rice
¼ cup green onion, chopped
¼ green or red bell pepper, chopped
1 cup marinated ulu "artichoke", chopped
1 tablespoon yellow curry
½ teaspoon salt
½ teaspoon black pepper
¾ cup mayonnaise
2 tablespoon Italian flat leaf parsley, chopped
(reserve 3 whole leaves for garnish)

Mix all ingredients together. Chill. Serve in a
large bowl lined with lettuce.

Makes a great appetizer served in individual
butter lettuce leaf bowls.

Ulu "Artichoke" Frittata

2 tablespoons olive oil
1 medium onion cut to ½ inch pieces
1 clove garlic crushed
½ small immature ulu, boiled and sliced
1 small zucchini sliced
1 cup fresh mushrooms sliced
1 cup Portuguese sausage sliced
       or ½ pound bacon
1-2 tablespoons olive oil
6 eggs slightly beaten
¼ cup cubed pepper jack cheese (or 2 slices
    veggie slices cheese)
2 tablespoons chopped Italian parsley
       and basil

In a separate pan, cook Portuguese sausage or bacon until browned. Drain and set aside.

Add olive oil to a large, heated cast iron pan (10-12 inches). Add onion and garlic, cook for 2-3 minutes. Do not burn garlic.   Add drained sausage, artichoke style ulu, zucchini and mushrooms, and sauté just until zucchini is bright green and mushrooms begin to soften, about 2-3 minutes. Sprinkle cheese over top of vegetables and immediately pour eggs over vegetables. Cook for 2-3 minutes until the bottom of eggs are firm. Place entire pan under broiler and broil for 3-5 minutes until top is fluffy and firm but not dry. To serve, run a spatula around edge of pan and invert onto a large plate and cut into wedges.

Ulu "Artichoke" Pasta Pesto Salad
A variation of a summer lunch favorite

12 ounces pasta*, boiled in salted water,
2 cooked immature green ulu, sliced
   Marinade:
        2 cloves garlic crushed
        ¼ cup white or rice vinegar
        ¼ cup light olive oil
        ¼ cup chopped white onion
        2 tablespoon fresh basil, chopped

½ cup ulu pesto (see page 21)
½ cup fresh green beans, blanched
½ cup broccoli florettes blanched
½ cup cherry tomatoes, cut in half and seeded
¼ cup red pepper
¼ cup celery
1 cup cooked garbanzo or red beans - optional
1/2 teaspoon salt
1/4 teaspoon

Marinate green ulu for at least 30 minutes. Mix with pesto and add vegetables cut into ¾ inch pieces. Toss in pasta, salt and pepper and chill.

* chilled firm cooked (penne, radiatore, campanelle)

Ulu "Artichoke" Pesto

1 immature green ulu, boiled, cut into pieces
3 cloves garlic
1 cup pine nuts
1/2 teaspoon salt
pinch black pepper
1/2 cup fresh basil leaves (Cuban or Sweet basil)
1 cup light olive oil (use in ½ cup portions)

Place garlic, pine nuts and basil into food processor bowl. Pulse and add first ½ cup olive oil slowly and process until smooth. Add ulu and pulse 3-4 times then process pouring olive oil slowly until desired consistency is reached.

Ulu "Artichokes" with Garlic

2 immature, green ulu
2 tablespoons olive oil
3 cloves garlic chopped
1 tablespoon capers
pepper to taste
splash dry wine

Boil whole immature ulu until fork tender, about 1 hour. Cut in half lengthwise and cut into thin wedges or about ¼ inch slices. Heat olive oil and garlic in a pan. Add sliced ulu cooking for 3-4 minutes. Add capers and finish with pepper and wine until heated through.

For a more traditional sauce, replace olive oil with butter.

22

Chapter 3

Side Dishes
Mature Ulu

 The ulu is Mature when the skin yellows and the milky sap comes though the skin. The bottom of the ulu may begin to brown but the stem will have white sap when picked. The ulu is hard all the way to the core.

The half ripe ulu when picked still feels firm on the outside but when sliced, the center is slightly soft and will have turned a light yellow. A mature ulu will ripen and soften in 1-3 days. Refrigeration will slow the process by about a day but the skin will turn dark brown.

Boiled or Steamed Ulu

Breadfruit can be boiled or steamed when it is whole or after it has been peeled and cut into pieces. Large pieces take longer to cook but they hold the full flavor of the ulu. Cooked Ulu tolerates freezing well. Raw ulu can also be frozen.

Candied Ulu
A variation of Candied Yams or Sweet Potatoes

3 cups mature ulu, cut into large chunks and
   boiled until tender
½ cup water or orange juice (or 1 medium orange
   sliced)
½ cup sugar
¼ teaspoon salt
2-3 tablespoons butter

In saucepan, combine sugar water and orange
juice. Simmer until sugar is dissolved. Add Ulu
and cook until sauce is thick and glazes ulu. Top
with 2-3 generous pats of butter and serve.

Alternative: Place in an ovenproof dish and top
with miniature marshmallows. Brown under
broiler before serving.

Chirashi Ulu

8 cups chopped ulu, cooked and drained well.
Sushi Seasoning –
Heat to a boil and allow to cool.
- 1 cup vinegar
- 2 tablespoons salt
- 2/3 cup sugar

Sushi – Gu -
- 2 tablespoons vegetable oil
- 2 tablespoons dried shrimp chopped fine
- 1 cup finely slivered carrots
- 1 cup finely sliced string beans
- 1 cup finely chopped shitake mushrooms (about 8 medium, soaked in warm water and chopped)
- ½ cup finely slivered gobo
- 2 tablespoons water
- 3 tablespoons sugar
- 1 tablespoon soy sauce
- 2 teaspoons salt
- 1 cup chopped kamaboko (umazaki)
- 2 eggs, lightly beaten and fried in a thin sheet, chopped.

Heat oil in a saucepan. Add dried shrimp, shitake, carrots, gobo and string beans. Add water (if needed), sugar, soy sauce and salt. Cook on high heat until just done. Add chopped kamaboko and chopped egg. Set aside and cool. Drain.

Toss cooked, chopped, well drained ulu. Sprinkle with vinegar mixture and mix gently. Add cooked vegetables to ulu mixture.

Crispy Ulu Baskets

4-5 cups coarsely shredded raw mature ulu
salt
oil for frying
4-5 inch metal sieves to mold baskets
(oil or spray with cooking spray)

Shred breadfruit using a large grater or large food processing plate. Shred about 1 to 1 ½ cups of breadfruit, enough to line one of the sieves. Place other sieve on top and press together. Submerge breadfruit in hot oil and fry until basket is golden brown and holds together as a basket. Remove from oil and let cool for a minute or 2 before removing. Use tongs…sieves will be very hot!

Repeat process shredding only enough breadfruit to make the next basket. (Soaking shredded breadfruit is not recommended as it is difficult to dry the breadfruit enough to prevent excessive hot oil splatter.

Baskets are fun individual containers for breakfast foods (scrambled eggs, sausage) or any time you want a unique presentation for a special buffet or lunch.

(potato)

Garlic Mashed Ulu
A variation of Garlic Mashed Potatoes

1 mature green ulu (4-5 cups)
2 teaspoons salt
½ - ¾ cup dairy or soy milk
¼ cup or ½ stick butter
½ teaspoon black pepper
2-3 cloves garlic, crushed

Wash, peel and core ulu. Cut into 2 inch chunks and boil in water until tender. Drain ulu in a colander. Mash ulu while hot with a potato masher. Add butter, salt, pepper, garlic and milk.

Grilled Ulu Chips

1 large mature ulu, peeled, cored and quartered
3 cloves garlic, crushed
¼ cup olive oil
salt to taste

Boil ulu covered in water until done but still firm, about 20 minutes. Slice ulu into 3/8 inch slices and marinate in olive oil and garlic. Place ulu slices on a hot grill. Grill until browned. Serve hot with a sprinkling of salt.

Mashed Ulu

Reminds me of mashed yellow potatoes

1 mature green ulu
2 tablespoon minced yellow onion
1 teaspoons salt
½ cup dairy or soy milk
4 tablespoons or ½ stick butter
½ teaspoon black pepper

Wash, peel and core ulu. Cut into 2 inch chunks boil in water until tender. Drain ulu and mash while hot with a potato masher. Add butter, onion (optional) salt, pepper, and milk.

Mazemeshi Ulu

8 cups chopped ulu, cooked, drained well

Gu - 2 tablespoons vegetable oil
     2 tablespoons dried shrimp chopped fine
     1 cup finely slivered carrots
     1 cup finely sliced string beans
     1 cup finely chopped shitake mushrooms
       (about 8 medium sized, soaked
         in warm water and chopped)
     ½ cup finely slivered gobo
     2 tablespoons water
     3 tablespoons sugar
     1 tablespoon soy sauce
     2 teaspoons salt
     1 cup chopped kamaboko (umazaki)
     2 eggs, lightly beaten and fried in a thin
       sheet, chopped.

Heat oil in a saucepan. Add dried shrimp, shitake, carrots, gobo and string beans. Add water (if needed), sugar, soy sauce and salt. Cook on high heat until just done. Add chopped kamaboko and chopped egg. Set aside and cool. Drain.

To make Mazemeshi ulu, toss cooked, chopped, well drained ulu. Add cooked vegetables to ulu, mixing gently.

Mushrooms Stuffed with Garlic Mashed Ulu
A garlic lovers favorite and meatless too

Mushroom caps:
1 pound large fresh mushrooms (about 12-15),
    stems removed
2 tablespoons each butter and olive oil
2 cloves garlic, crushed

Filling:
3 cups boiled or steamed ulu, mashed
3 large cloves garlic, crushed or finely minced.
¼ cup or ½ block butter
½ cup milk (soy or dairy)
chopped mushroom stems, (cooked in butter)
Salt and pepper to taste
2 tablespoons fresh Italian flat parsley

Remove stems from large caps and chop. Cook mushroom caps in butter, olive oil and garlic until browned on each side. Remove caps from pan.

Cook chopped mushroom stems in pan. Add remaining filling ingredients. Fill each mushroom cap generously. Place on cookie sheet and broil until tops are lightly browned and heated through (5 to 10 minutes). Large mushroom caps can be baked at 375 degrees until heated through and tops are brown (15 to 20 minutes).

Variation: - Substitute 2 to 3 tablespoons minced
                  garlic chives for garlic in filling.
              - Substitute 2 tablespoons chopped
                  Rosemary or Thyme for Italian
                  Parsley

Portuguese Style Twice Cooked Ulu

1 medium green, mature Ulu, boiled, cut into 1-
    inch wedges
4 tablespoons or ½ stick butter
4 tablespoons olive oil
1 clove garlic crushed
½ cup chopped coriander (Chinese or Mexican
    Parsley)
Salt and pepper to taste

Heat butter, oil and garlic in a heavy bottom pan.
Add Ulu and cook until brown. Toss with salt,
fresh ground pepper and chopped coriander and
serve.

Alternate: Toss all ingredients together in a
baking pan. Cover with foil and bake in oven for
30 minutes at 350 degrees. Remove foil just
before serving and bake until brown.

Roasted Ulu with Garlic

1 green mature ulu, cut into 2 inch chunks
3-4 cloves garlic, crushed
2 tablespoons olive oil
½ teaspoon ground black pepper
½ cup water

Wash, core and peel breadfruit. Toss with crushed garlic and olive oil. Place in a baking pan with 1 cup water. Cover pan with foil. Bake for 1 hour at 325 degrees, removing foil after 45 minutes, stirring occasionally to brown evenly. Salt to taste before serving.

For Onion ulu, add 1 cup chopped onion in place of garlic.

Roasted Ulu with Olives

1 medium Ulu boiled, cut into 3/4 inch wedges.
½ cup olive oil
2 large cloves garlic crushed
½ cup chopped or sliced olives (green, Calamata or black)
½ cup water
½ cup chopped Italian flat parsley

Toss Ulu wedges in olive oil, garlic, salt and pepper. Place in a pan with ½ cup water. Cover with foil and bake at 350 degrees for 60 minutes. Remove cover after 30 minutes and continue baking until golden brown. Turn ulu to brown evenly. Toss with olives and parsley just before serving (return to oven for 5 minutes to warm through).

Scalloped Ulu
A variation of a potato classic

4-5 cups mature green breadfruit, sliced and
    boiled until tender
½ cup onion, sliced thin
1 clove garlic

White Sauce:
>   4 tablespoons butter
>   3 tablespoons flour
>   2 cups dairy or soy milk
>   1 teaspoon salt
>   ¼ teaspoon pepper

In a heavy bottom or non–stick pan, heat butter and flour mixing constantly to form a paste (roux). Cook for 2-3 minutes until cooked but not brown. Slowly add milk, salt and pepper using a whisk, until smooth. Sauce will appear thin. Do not boil.

In large dutch oven, heat oil, add onions, garlic and breadfruit. Heat through and add white sauce. Pour into a 9 by 13 inch pan, sprayed with cooking spray. Cover with foil. Bake in a 350 degree over for about 60 minutes. Remove cover during last 15 minutes to brown.

Optional: Top with toasted breadcrumbs, or potato chips before serving.

Scalloped Ulu with Cheese
A variation of a potato classic

4-5 cups mature green breadfruit, sliced and
   boiled until tender
½ cup onion, sliced thin
2 cloves garlic
½ cup bell pepper (optional)

White Sauce:
   4 tablespoons butter
   3 tablespoons flour
   2 cups dairy or soy milk
   1 teaspoon salt
   ¼ teaspoon pepper
   1 cup shredded white (mozzarella, jack or
      ½ cup parmesan)

In a heavy bottom or non-stick pan, heat butter
and flour, mixing to form a paste (roux). Cook for
2-3 minutes until cooked but not brown. Slowly
add milk, salt and pepper using a whisk, until
smooth.   Sauce will appear thin. Mix in shredded
cheese. Do not boil.

In large Dutch oven, heat oil, add onions, garlic
and breadfruit.   Heat through and add white
sauce. Pour into a 9 by 13 inch pan, sprayed with
cooking spray. Cover with foil. Bake in a 350
degree over for about 60 minutes. Remove cover
during last 15 minutes to brown.

Optional: Top with toasted breadcrumbs, or
potato chips before serving.

(pumpkin)
Shoyu Sugar Ulu
Adapted from an oriental classic

1 medium mature (green or half ripe) breadfruit
2 cups water
½ cup shoyu
1/3 to 1/2 cup white or brown sugar

Peel, quarter and core breadfruit. Cut into 2-3 inch chunks. Steam in water until ulu is almost done.(15-20 minutes) Add shoyu and sugar and cook over low heat until ulu is tender. Stir often to prevent burning. Add more water if ulu becomes too sticky.

(sweet potato)
Sweet Ulu Chips

1 half ripe mature ulu
Oil for deep-frying
Salt

Peel and core ulu. Cut into thin slices and soak in water to prevent browning. Drain sliced ulu and pat dry. Fry on medium heat until light brown. Salt to taste.

The half ripe fruit is higher in sugar than the green fruit and may brown quickly.

Try a light sprinkling of salt and sugar for a "kettle corn" like flavor.

(sweet potato)

Ulu and Shrimp Tempura

2 cups cooked sweet or half ripe ulu
10 large shrimp
½ cup raw fish cake
¼ teaspoon salt
1 teaspoon sugar
long rice, cut into short pieces

Cut ulu into ½ inch thick slices then break into 2 to 3 inch wide chunks. Shell shrimp and chop fine or mash. Combine shrimp with fish cake, add salt and sugar and mix until it forms a paste. Coat breadfruit with a thin layer of shrimp and fishcake paste. Roll in long rice. Drop into hot oil and deep fry until light brown. Drain on paper towel and serve.

Ulu Chips

1 green, mature ulu
Oil for deep-frying
Salt

Peel and core ulu. Cut into thin slices and soak in water to prevent browning. Drain sliced ulu and pat dry. Fry on medium-high heat until light brown. Salt to taste.

Ulu chips are crunchier than potato chips. They make great dip chips!

Alternative: Replace salt with garlic salt.

Ulu Dinner Fries

1 mature green breadfruit
1 chili pepper
1 clove garlic
salt (or garlic salt)
oil for frying

Peel, quarter and remove core from firm breadfruit. Boil until cooked but not quite tender about 20 minutes with whole chili pepper and sliced garlic. Drain and let pieces air dry until cool enough to handle. Discard chili pepper and garlic.

Heat oil in a medium sized pot with 2-3 inches of oil on medium heat.

Slice breadfruit in to 3/8 inch thick slices. Cook in hot oil until edges begin to brown. Remove from oil and drain on paper towel. Salt to taste (Garlic salt is great too). Do not cook until completely golden brown, as slices will become very hard.

Serve hot as "dinner fries". These are great dipping fries and remind me of those thick "coffee shop" French fries my sister used to love to eat, covered in ketchup.

Ulu Hash Browns

3 cups coarsely shredded mature green ulu
½ medium round onion (about ½ cup) chopped
¼ cup water
salt and pepper to taste
oil for frying

Mix together shredded ulu and chopped onion with salt a pepper. Heat large cast iron Skillet or a non–stick frying pan. Add 2 to 3 tablespoons olive oil when pan is hot. Add seasoned ulu and onions to pan. Add ¼ cup water and let steam for 5-10 minutes with the pan covered. When ulu begins to soften, remove cover and press down on the ulu with a spatula.

When the bottom of the ulu begins to brown (about 15-20 minutes) and starts to hold together, divide the ulu into 4 wedges. Turn each wedge when golden brown. Remove from pan when golden brown and crispy on both sides.

Serve with plenty of Ketchup and Hot sauce.

Ulu Inarizushi
Cone sushi

Cones for Sushi
- 2 packages aburage, 4 pieces each
- ½ cup water
- 2 Tablespoons sake (optional)
- 2 tablespoons sugar or 4 packets Splenda tm
- 1 teaspoon salt
- 1 teaspoon soy sauce

Chirashi Ulu (see recipe on page 24)

Soak aburage in hot water to soften. Drain and cut each triangle aburage in half to make 2 triangles. If using rectangle pieces, make a slit along long side of rectangle. Open pocked gently. Cook in water, sake, sugar, salt and soy sauce mixture for 10 minutes. Set aside and cool.

To assemble Inarizushi, Squeeze excess liquid from aburage cones. Stuff Chirashi Ulu.

Ulu Shoestring "Potatoes"

1 mature green ulu, peeled, cored and sliced into
   ¼ inch shoestrings
oil for frying
salt

Slice ulu into ¼ inch strings. Soak in cold water. Drain ulu well and pat dry before frying. Drop by small handfuls into oil, separating strands (Chinese wire strainer works well). Fry until crisp. Drain on paper towels. Salt to taste and serve.

Great with ketchup and black pepper or hot sauce.

Ulu Stuffing

For those who like Chestnut stuffing, try this using half ripe, slightly sweet Ulu

1 loaf bread, wheat or white bread (about 4
   cups cubes)
1 pound bacon
1 tablespoon light olive oil
1 tablespoon butter
1 medium onion chopped
2 stalks celery chopped fine
3 cloves garlic minced or crushed
2 cups mature or half ripe ulu, cubed
1 tablespoon fresh basil and thyme
½ tablespoon fresh rosemary
1 cup water or chicken stock
½ teaspoon salt (to taste)
½ teaspoon ground black pepper

Break bread into ½ to ¾ inch pieces or cut into cubes with a serrated knife. Spread in a single layer on a cookie sheet and allow to dry. Slice bacon, and cook until almost crisp. Drain oil. Add olive oil, butter, vegetables and garlic. Cook until translucent. Add ulu and herbs, salt, pepper and broth. Simmer for 5-10 minutes. Add bread and stir well to combine. Reduce heat and cook until heated through.

Ulu with Cheese Stuffed Mushrooms

Sauté in a large heavy bottom pan:
1 pound large stuffing mushrooms (about 12-15)
2 tablespoons butter
2 tablespoons olive oil
1 clove garlic, crushed

Filling:
3 cups boiled or steamed ulu, mashed
½ medium round onion, minced (about ¼ cup) or
    ¼ cup chopped green onion
½ block or ¼ cup butter
½ cup milk (soy or regular)
½ cup grated cheese (or 3 slices Veggie slices tm,
broken into small pieces)
chopped mushroom stems (optional)
Salt and pepper to taste

Remove stems from large caps. Add garlic to
heated butter and olive oil in an oven proof pan.
Do not burn garlic. Brown mushrooms lightly on
each side. Remove mushroom caps from pan and
set aside until cool enough to handle.

Lightly cook chopped mushroom stems. Mash
ulu, adding butter milk, salt and pepper, stirring in
mushroom stem pieces and cheese last. Fill each
mushroom cap generously.   Place on cookie
sheet and broil lightly until tops are lightly
browned and heated through (5-10 minutes)   If
mushroom caps are very large, bake at 375
degrees until heated through and tops are brown
(15-20 minutes).

Chapter 4

Breads and Noodles
Mature

Ulu Peroiges

Ulu Handling Tips

To make the breadfruit, ulu, easier to peel , cut a thin slice off the stem end and off the bottom. Stand the ulu on the flat spot. Cut a thin slice of skin, cutting down the side of the fruit. Turn the ulu after each slice of skin is removed. Continue around the ulu until peeled. Dip the ulu in water every few slices to keep it from browning.

To core the ulu, cut the ulu in half lengthwise and again in quarters. Trim out the core from the stem end, cutting toward the center of the ulu.

The ulu browns as soon as it is cut. Soaking ulu in water will keep it from turning brown. This also reduces build up of the sticky sap on utensils. Cooking oil or spray helps to remove the sticky latex from utensils.

(potato)
Plain Ulu Biscuits

Sift:

    2 cups all purpose or whole wheat pastry
        flour
    2 teaspoons baking powder
    1 teaspoon baking soda
    1 Tablespoon sugar
    ½ teaspoon salt

Cut into flour mixture:
    4 tablespoons butter

Mix in a bowl:
    ¾ cup cooked, mashed mature ulu
    ¾ cup dairy or soy milk

Preheat oven to 450 degrees. Spray cookie sheet with cooking spray. Sift flour, baking powder, sugar and salt. Cut butter into flour. In a separate bowl, mix ulu and milk.

Make a well in dry ingredients and add wet ingredients all at once. Use your hand and mix quickly until the dough makes a ball on your hand. Scrape dough out onto a floured board and knead just a few turns until dough holds together. Press dough shaping it to ½ inch thick. Cut with a biscuit cutter or cup. Place on baking sheet and bake for 10-12 minutes, lowering heat to 400 degrees.

Alternate: Press dough into a ½ inch thick rectangle. Cut into 12 pieces, using a floured pastry scraper (like scones). Bake as above.

Ulu Kugel

1 medium mature green or half ripe ulu, peeled,
    cored and coarsely grated (5 -6 cups grated)
2 large onions, chopped
12 eggs, beaten
1 cup matzo meal (may substitute dry bread
    crumbs or cracker crumbs)
½ teaspoon salt
pepper to taste

¼ cup vegetable oil or cooking spray

Mix grated ulu, onions, beaten eggs and matzo
meal to make a batter. Add salt and pepper.

Heat a 9 by 13 inch baking pan in a 350 degree
oven for 5 minutes. Spray with cooking spray or
pour half of the oil into the bottom of the pan,
spreading evenly. Pour batter into pan. Spread
remaining oil evenly over top of batter or spray
with cooking spray. Bake for 30-40 minutes until
golden brown. Cut into generous squares and
serve.

(potato)
Ulu Latke
Ulu Story: My friend Geetal taught me how to make these in her kitchen in Anahola. Jewish potato pancakes with ulu.

3-4 cups mature green ulu grated (soak grated
    ulu in water)
1 teaspoon salt
¼ teaspoon black pepper
3-4 tablespoons flour
1 large egg
Oil for frying

Topping: Sour Cream and Apple Sauce

Drain ulu well in colander, shaking out excess water. Add salt, pepper and egg to grated Ulu. Sprinkle with flour to make a very light batter to coat ulu.

Heat a heavy bottom frying pan (cast iron) and add about 1/8 inch of oil on the bottom. Place rounded tablespoons in pan and flatten to 3-4 inch circles. Fry until golden brown on each side.

Drain on absorbent paper. Serve with Sour Cream and Apple Sauce.

Alternative: Add about 1/2 cup chopped onion to ulu before frying, Serve with Sour Cream and fresh green onions or chives.

Ulu Lavosh
A variation of a Middle Eastern classic

Mix dry ingredients and cut in butter:
   3 cups flour
   ½ teaspoon baking soda
   1 teaspoon salt
   2 tablespoons sugar
   ½ cup butter (1 block)

Add:
   1 cup buttermilk (1 tablespoon vinegar and
      add dairy or soy milk to make 1 cup)
   1 ¼ cups mashed ulu

6 Tablespoons sesame seeds

Add milk and mashed ulu mixture to dry ingredients. Dough will be slightly sticky. Form dough into 8-10 small balls. Coat each ball with sesame seeds. Roll dough out thin on a floured board. Bake on an ungreased cookie sheet for 10-15 minutes in a 400 degree preheated oven.

Cool on a wire rack until crisp. Return to oven for 5-10 minutes if crackers are not crispy once cooled. Store in an airtight container.

Serve with softened butter or herbed cream cheese spread.

Ulu Noodles

2 cups mashed cooked mature ulu
2 eggs
2 cups flour
1 ½ teaspoons salt

Mix mashed ulu, egg and flour. Turn onto a floured board. Knead until smooth using a pastry scraper. Dough will be moist and slightly sticky. Let rest in an oiled bowl for 30 minutes.

Roll out on floured board until about 1/8 inch thick. Flour well and loosely roll dough. Slice into ¼ to ½ inch wide noodles. Loosen noodles. Drop into boiling water for 2-3 minutes until done (but still firm). Do not over cook.

These noodles are the "thick" home made kind, found in old-fashioned chicken noodle soup. For cold noodle dishes, chill in ice water to keep noodles firm. Drain noodles as soon as they are cold.

Ulu Pancakes

1 cup cooked half ripe or ripe ulu, chopped
2 cups flour
1 ½ teaspoons baking powder
1 ½ teaspoons baking soda
½ teaspoon salt
2 Tablespoon sugar
2 eggs
¾ cup dairy or soy milk plus 1 tablespoon vinegar
(or buttermilk)
2 Tablespoons oil

Mix dry ingredients, sifting baking powder, baking
soda and salt. Add egg, milk mixture and oil to
make a batter. Add ulu, separating pieces while
mixing. Let batter rest for 5 minutes before
cooking. Drop onto a medium hot griddle, turning
when top is covered with bubbles. Serve with
butter and Maple Syrup or Guava Jam.

(potato)
Ulu Pierogies

Noodle Dough: Mix together:
1 cup mashed cooked mature ulu (like potato)
1 egg
1 cup flour
1 teaspoon salt

Turn onto a floured board. Knead until smooth using a pastry scraper. Dough will be moist and sticky. Let rest in an oiled bowl for 30 minutes. Prepare filling while dough is resting.

Cabbage filling: Heat oil in pan. Add onions and garlic, cooking until soft. Add cabbage and cook until wilted. Squeeze out excess liquid.
   2 tablespoons
   3 cups shredded cabbage, kale or collards or 3
      cups spinach)
   4 cloves garlic crushed
   ½ cup round onion chopped fine
   ½ teaspoon salt
   ¼ teaspoon pepper

Divide dough into walnut sized pieces. On a floured surface, roll dough into a 3½ to 4 inch circle.   Fill dough with a rounded spoonful of filling.   Fold dough over and moisten edges of dough with water if needed.   Pinch edges together firmly. Drop Pierogies into boiling water (about 5 minutes). Remove and drain. Heat butter or oil in a large skillet. Brown Pierogies on both sides. Makes 10-12 dumplings.

Garlic Mashed Ulu Filling

2 ½ cups boiled ulu, mashed
4 cloves garlic, crushed or 2 tablespoons garlic
    chives, chopped
1 teaspoon salt
¼ teaspoon pepper

Mash ulu while warm. Add garlic, salt and
pepper.

For traditional "potato cheese" filling, use mashed
ulu above, omit garlic, add ¼ cup finely minced
onion and 1 cup shredded cheese.

Mushroom Filling

2 cups cooked ulu, mashed
2 cups chopped mushrooms
2 tablespoons oil
¼ cup chopped onion
3 cloves garlic

Cook onions, garlic and mushrooms and onions in
oil until soft. Drain well, mash with cooked ulu.

(banana)
Ulu Quick Bread

1 cup (2 sticks) butter, softened
1 cup sugar
4 eggs
2 teaspoons vanilla

Sift together dry ingredients::
  4 cups flour
  1 tablespoon baking powder
  ½ teaspoon salt
  ½ cup finely chopped macadamia nuts
      or almonds, optional

Mix together:
  2 ½ cups ripe ulu pulp
  1 tablespoon baking soda
  1 cup milk (soy or dairy) + 1 tablespoon
      vinegar

In a separate bowl, mix ulu pulp with baking soda. Add the milk and vinegar mixture. Set aside to allow mixture to develop fine bubbles.

In a large bowl, cream softened butter and sugar. Add eggs and vanilla. Stir in dry ingredients. Before batter is completely blended, add ulu pulp mixture.

Grease and flour the bottom of 2, 9 X 5 inch loaf pans. Pour batter into pan and bake at 350 degrees for about 60 minutes. Bread will pull away from sides of pan when done.

Sweet Ulu Biscuits

Sift together:
    2 cups flour
    2 teaspoons baking powder
    1 teaspoon baking soda
    1 tablespoon sugar
    ½ teaspoon salt

Cut into flour mixture:
    2 tablespoons butter

Mix in a bowl:
    1 cup cooked, mashed ripe (sweet) ulu
    ½ cup dairy or soy milk
    ½ cup raisins or dried fruit, optional

Preheat oven to 450 degrees. Spray cookie sheet with cooking spray. Sift flour, baking powder, baking soda, sugar and salt. Cut butter into flour mixture. In a separate bowl, mix ripe ulu and milk.

Make a "well" in flour and butter mixture and pour milk and ulu mixture into "well" all at once. Using your hand and mix quickly until the dough forms a ball on your hand. Scrape dough out onto a floured board and knead just a few turns until it holds together. Press dough shaping it, ½ inch thick. Cut with a 3 inch biscuit cutter or cup. Place on baking sheet and lower oven temperature to 400 degrees. Bake for 10-12 minutes until light brown.

Serve with soft butter and jam, or honey.

Chapter 5

Soups and Salads
Mature

Ulu with Sun Dried Tomatoes and Capers

This is a meal of a salad...it also has chunks of chicken, red pepper and olives.

Codfish Ulu Salad
A variation of a Puerto Rican Specialty

1 cup shredded codfish soaked and drained
2 cups cooked warabi (fiddle head fern shoots)
2 cups cooked, green mature ulu
1 medium tomato diced
1 medium sweet onion sliced thin
2 teaspoons soy sauce or patis

Soak codfish in water until excess salt is removed. Drain and set aside. Boil warabi for 5 to 8 minutes in salted water. Drain and plunge warabi in iced water to stop cooking and to make warabi crispy. Slice warabi into 1 to 2 inch pieces. Cut ulu and tomato into ½ inch cubes. Cut sweet onion into thin slices. Toss all ingredients together and chill before serving.

Creamy Ulu Kale Soup
A variation of Classic Cream of Broccoli

1 medium onion, chopped
2 tablespoons olive oil
3 cloves garlic minced or crushed
2 stalks celery chopped
3 cups mature, green ulu cut into 1 inch cubes
1 ½ cups soy or diary milk
2 cups stock (veggie or chicken) or water
1-2 teaspoons salt
¼ teaspoon black pepper
1 teaspoon fresh thyme optional
1 bunch kale (about 12 leaves) stems removed

In a large pot, heat oil on medium heat. Add onion, garlic and celery and cook until transparent, do not brown. Add ulu cubes and stock or water. Simmer until ulu is tender, about 20-30 minutes. Add salt and pepper and thyme to taste. Remove from heat. Using a potato masher, mash ulu in pot until soup is thick. Return to heat finishing soup adding chopped kale leaves, cooking for 2 to 3 minutes, adding soy or dairy milk last. Heat soup through but do not boil.

To make soup thicker, remove 2 cups from pot and blend until smooth and return to pot.

Alternatives: Substitute Broccoli ... about ½ pound; Carrot chunks and a tiny bit of curry make for a hearty winter soup.

(potato)
Hot German Style Ulu Salad
A variation of a German Classic

3 to 4 cups mature cooked ulu, cut into chunks
1 pound bacon
2 tablespoons sugar
1 heaping teaspoon flour
½ cup white vinegar
½ cup water
1 medium onion diced
½ teaspoon black pepper

Fry bacon, drain (reserve 2 tablespoon bacon fat) and crumble. Set aside.

Heat bacon fat and add sugar, vinegar, flour and water over medium heat until sugar is dissolved. Add onions and cook for 2-3 minutes. Season with pepper. Toss dressing with ulu and ½ of the bacon. Sprinkle remainder of bacon to top to salad.

Hot Seafood Salad
A variation of a party favorite

6 cups mature green ulu, boiled and cooled
½ pound fresh shrimp or 2 flat cans shrimp,
 drained
½ pound fresh fish
2 flat cans crab meat, drained
4 ounces shredded imitation crab
1 medium onion, chopped
2 stalks celery chopped
1/2 cup mayonnaise
1/2 block butter melted
¼ teaspoon black pepper
3-4 drops of liquid hot pepper sauce (optional)

Clean and cut fresh seafood into ¾ inch pieces.
Cook onions and celery in butter until softened.
Add fresh seafood and cook for 3 to 4 minutes.
Add remaining ingredients except ulu and
mayonnaise and heat through. Combine ulu,
mayonnaise and seafood mixture. Pour into a 9
by 13 pan and bake at 450 degrees for 20-25
minutes until heated through and top is lightly
browned.

Ulu Noodle Soup
Chicken noodle soup

1 recipe Ulu Noodles (see page 49)

1 whole Chicken
2 tablespoon oil
4 cups water or stock
3 cloves garlic
2 medium onions, chopped
2 stalks celery, chopped
2 medium carrots, cut into ½ inch cubes
2 teaspoons salt
½ teaspoon pepper
1 teaspoon fresh thyme, optional

Brown chicken with garlic in a heavy bottom pot.
Discard excess oil. Add water and heat to boiling.
Cook chicken for about 30 minutes or until tender.
While chicken is cooking, make ulu noodles.

Remove chicken from pot and set aside to cool.
Skim oil from chicken stock. Remove skin and
bones from chicken.

Add onions, celery and carrots to chicken stock
and cook until vegetables are tender. Add thyme.
Return chicken chunks and boiled ulu noodles to
soup. Simmer for 5 minutes to heat chicken and
noodles through.

Ulu "Potato" Salad

4 cups boiled, cubed mature ulu
1 stalk celery minced
½ medium onion, minced
¼ teaspoon black pepper
1 teaspoon salt
1 ¼ cups mayonnaise
2 heaping tablespoons sweet pickle relish or dill
     pickle relish
¼ cup grated carrot (or 1 flat can crab meat,
     drained)
½ cup frozen peas (or 1 cup sliced cucumber
     salted and squeezed well)
2 hard boiled eggs, chopped

Add chopped onion, celery, salt and pepper to ulu
while it is hot. Toss to coat well, set aside until
cool. Add remaining ingredients, mix well and
chill. Microwave peas briefly to heat through or
drop for 1 minute in boiling water. Refresh in cold
water and drain well.

Alternatives:
Instead of mayonnaise, red wine vinegar and oil
(half and half mix) makes a lighter salad.

Ulu Clam Chowder

2 medium onions chopped
2 tablespoons olive oil
3 to 4 cloves garlic minced or crushed
2 stalks celery chopped
½ small green bell pepper chopped
4 cups mature, green ulu cut into ¾ inch cubes
5 cans chopped clams with juice
2 cups soy or diary milk
2 cups water
1 teaspoons salt
½ teaspoon black pepper
2 tablespoons fresh thyme
1 tablespoon fresh rosemary chopped
2 tablespoons chopped Italian parsley (reserve
few whole leaves for garnish)

In a large pot, heat oil on medium heat. Add
onion, garlic and celery, ½ of the herb mixture
and cook until onions are transparent, do not
brown.   Add ulu cubes, and stock or water.
Simmer until ulu is tender, about 20 to 30
minutes.   Remove 2 cups of the ulu and
vegetables and blend in blender or mash with
potato masher. Return to pot.   Add clams with
juice and remaining herbs.   Add salt, pepper to
taste. Finish soup adding soy or dairy milk. Heat
soup through but do not boil. Serve with a whole
parsley leaf and a grating of fresh pepper.

Additions: ½ pound bacon, chopped an cooked,
excess fat drained, add with onions;
1 small carrot chopped if you like a slightly sweet
chowder.

  Ulu Clam Chowder – *continued*

Any mix of seafood works very well, frozen seafood mixes are convenient

Whole fresh clams make wonderful chowder. Steam them separately just until they open then add the whole clams carefully to the soup near the end of cooking. Add the remaining clam juice, being careful of any sand or grit, which may have settled, in the steaming liquid.

For Tomato based **Manhattan Style Chowder**

Instead of 2 cups milk, add a 12 ounce can of diced tomato and an 8 ounce can of tomato sauce with the ulu cubes. Cook as above.

(potato)
Ulu Corn Chowder

1 medium onion chopped
½ pound bacon, cut into ½ inch slices
1 clove garlic minced or crushed
2 stalks celery chopped
2 cups mature, green ulu cut into3/4 inch cubes
1 large can, about 12 ounces, creamed corn
1 ½ cups soy or diary milk
2 cups soup stock (vegetable or chicken) or water
1-2 teaspoons salt
¼ teaspoon black pepper
1 teaspoon fresh thyme optional

In a large pot, cook bacon, drain excess oil. Add onion, garlic and celery and cook until transparent, do not brown. Add ulu cubes and stock or water. Simmer until ulu is tender, about 20-30 minutes. Add salt and pepper and thyme to taste. Remove from heat. Using an old-fashioned potato masher, mash ulu in pot until soup is thick. Return to heat finishing soup adding creamed corn, cooking for 2-3 minutes, adding soy or dairy milk. Heat soup through but do not boil.

For thicker chowder, remove 2 cups from pot and blend until smooth and return to pot.

(potato)
Ulu Vegan Vegetable Soup

2 cups, cooked ulu, cut into 1 inch cubes
4 tablespoons olive oil
4 cloves garlic crushed
1 block tofu, cut into 1 inch cubes drained well
1 large onion, cut into ½ inch cubes
2 stalks celery cut into ½ inch pieces
1 14 ounce canned, diced, tomato (do not drain)
    plus 1 can water
2 medium carrots
1 cup broccoli, peeled and sliced
1 cup cauliflower cut into pieces
1 medium zucchini
¼ medium cabbage (or 6 collard leaves sliced)
1 cup green string beans
1 12 ounce can garbanzo beans
1 cup frozen corn (optional)
1 bay leaf
1 tablespoon fresh thyme or basil
1 teaspoon fresh oregano or rosemary, optional
½ cup Italian flat parsley chopped
Salt and pepper to taste

Heat oil in large saucepan. Add tofu, turning each piece to brown all sides. Add garlic, cooking until fragrant. Add onions, celery and carrots. Add diced tomatoes and remaining ingredients. Add ulu. Simmer for 20 minutes or until vegetables are tender. To give your soup the "cooked all day flavor", remove 2 cups of vegetables and soup. Blend and return to pot.

(potato)
Ulu Vegetable Soup

1 pound (about 1 ½ cups) chicken or beef
2 cups cooked ulu, cut into ½ inch cubes
2 tablespoons olive oil
1 large onion, cubed
2 stalks celery cut into ½ inch pieces
2 cloves garlic crushed
1 14 ounce canned, diced tomato (do not drain)
   plus 1 can water
2 medium carrots
1 cup broccoli, peeled and sliced
1 cup cauliflower cut into pieces
1 medium zucchini
¼ medium cabbage (or 6 collard leaves sliced)
1 cup green string beans
1 12 ounce can garbanzo beans
1 cup frozen corn (optional)
1 Bay leaf
1 teaspoon fresh thyme or rosemary, optional
1 teaspoon salt
¼ teaspoon pepper

Heat oil in large saucepan and brown beef or chicken. Add onions, celery and garlic and cook until fragrant. Add diced tomatoes and remaining ingredients. Add ulu. Simmer for 20 minutes or until all vegetables are tender.

To give your soup the cooked all day flavor, remove 2 cups of vegetables and soup. Blend and return to pot.

Ulu Chicken Salad with Capers
And Sun Dried Tomatoes

Ulu Story: This is "Julie's Salad". Her neighbor made this salad for her last year and it was so popular, we wanted the recipe. Her neighbor told her how to make it, just telling her what to put in it, with no specific quantities.   My favorite "measurement" was half a bottle of capers…when asked what size bottle, the reply was "the regular size bottle".

1 medium ulu, cut into wedges
    Boil in water to cover with:
        6 cloves crushed garlic
        2 chili peppers
        2 tablespoons Hawaiian salt (rock salt)
        2 tablespoons oil
        3 tablespoons vinegar
        2 sprigs fresh dill (optional)

½ cup sweet onion, sliced thin
¼ teaspoon black pepper
1 teaspoon salt
3 large chicken breasts, grilled, skin removed
1 ¼ cups mayonnaise
2 heaping tablespoons dill pickle relish
1 can small olives, drained
12 sun dried tomato halves, cut into quarters
¾ cup red bell pepper cut into ½ inch pieces
3 heaping tablespoons capers
¼ cup green onion

Cut cooked ulu into ¾ inch pieces (about 8 cups) Add sliced sweet onion, salt and pepper to ulu while it is hot. Toss and set aside until cool. Cook chicken breasts and allow to cool. Cut into 1 inch chunks (3 cups). Mix all remaining ingredients together. Chill before serving.

Chapter 6

Main Dishes
Mature

Kim Chee "Fried Rice" Style Ulu

Main Dishes
(potato)

Baked Stuffed Ulu
"twice baked" potatoes pacific style

Ulu Story: I met a woman at our local library and she told me about the first time she tasted ulu. When she moved to Kauai years ago, she went camping with a friend. She told me of how the ulu was roasted on the campfire and when it was cooked, it was split open filled with cheese and salt and pepper. The halves were placed back together, and the ulu was returned to the fire until warmed and served scooped from the halves.

Place in baking pan and bake 350 degrees:
- 1 green mature ulu
- 2 tablespoons olive oil
- ¼ teaspoon ground black pepper
- 1 cup water

Scoop out ulu and mash with:
- 1/2 teaspoon salt
- ½ cup or 1 block butter
- 1 cup shredded cheese
- 2 tablespoons finely minced green onion
- (or Italian flat parsley or Garlic chives)

Cut ulu in half and rub cut side with olive oil and black pepper. Place in a baking pan with 1 cup water, cut side down. Cover pan with foil. Bake for 1 hour until easily pierced with a fork.

Remove Ulu from oven. Scoop ulu pulp, leaving a ½ thick shell. Mash ulu with butter and onions. Return mashed Ulu to shells and place in baking pan. Bake at 350 degrees uncovered until heated through and tops are brown.

Alternative: Soy cheese works well.

(potato)
Chicken Adobo with Ulu

1 whole chicken, cut into pieces
Marinate in:
> 3 cloves garlic
> 2 bay leaves
> 3 pieces ginger
> 3 tablespoons shoyu (soy sauce)
> 4 tablespoons vinegar

2 tablespoons oil
½ cup water
3 cups boiled ulu, cut into 2 inch pieces.

Braise chicken in oil until brown. Return marinade to pot. Add water and simmer for 45 minutes. Add ulu and cook until ulu is tender and browned.

(taro)
Chinese Style Ulu Cakes
A variation of a Chinese Dim Sum favorite

4 cups boiled mature green ulu
½ pound lup chong, chopped
4 stalks green onion chopped
2 teaspoons salt

Brown lup chong and drain oil. Mix all ingredients and place in a 9X9 pan, lined with Ti leaf or Banana leaf. Place a large pan in the oven and fill with water ½ inch deep. Place the 9X9 pan in the larger baking pan and bake in a 350-degree oven for 60 minutes. Remove from oven and cool for a few minutes before slicing into 2x3 inch diamonds. *1 cup cooked Char Siu pork or shrimp are great additions.

Kimchee Fried Rice Style Ulu

6 cups chopped raw ulu, boiled until cooked but
   still firm
10 ounces or 2 cups chopped Char Sui, Lup
   Chong or Portuguese Sausage
1 medium or 1 cup chopped round onion
1 clove garlic crushed
2 stalks green onion chopped
1 cup kim chee, squeezed and chopped
2 to 3 tablespoons oil
2 tablespoons soy sauce
3 stalks green onion chopped
½ teaspoon salt
¼ teaspoon pepper
2 large eggs, lightly beaten

Drain boiled chopped ulu and set aside. Heat
heavy bottom pan and brown chopped meat.
Drain excess oil if necessary and add crushed
garlic, round onion and kim chee. Add 2-3
tablespoons oil to the pan to keep ulu from
sticking. Add drained ulu and season with soy
sauce, salt and pepper. When ulu is browned,
make a well in the center of the mixture. Pour
egg into center of the well and allow to cook until
it just begins to set. Scramble egg, mixing it
throughout the ulu mixture. Add green onion just
before serving.

* Raw Ulu chunks can be pulsed in a food
processor until pea sized.

For a restaurant style treat, top each serving with
a fried egg.

(potato)
New England Boiled Dinner

2 to 3 pounds Corned Beef
2 onions cut each in half
4 cups mature ulu, cut into 1½ inch wedges
4 stalks celery cut in half
4 large carrots, peeled, cut in half
1 head cabbage, cut into thick wedges
Salt and pepper to taste

Cover Corned Beef with water and simmer for ½ hour. Discard water. Add fresh water and bring to a simmer, 1 to 2 hours until tender. Add vegetables except cabbage. When carrots and ulu are fork tender, add cabbage. Add salt and pepper to taste.

Remove Corned beef from broth and allow to rest for 15 minutes before slicing. Serve on a large platter with vegetables arranged around corned beef slices. Serve with yellow or brown spicy mustard.

Alternative: Add fresh corn on the cob to pot, and steam on top of broth for 5 minutes. Remove corn and serve on a large platter

Portuguese Style Boiled Dinner with Ulu

2 pounds pork (with bone)
2 cans garbanzo beans, drained (or one cup dried
beans soaked over night)
1 pound Portuguese sausage
1 onion, cut into wedges
3 cups mature ulu, cut into 1 ½ inch chunks
1 pound kale chopped or cabbage
1 cup elbow macaroni
Salt and pepper to taste

Cover pork with water and simmer for 1 hour until
tender. Skim broth as needed. Cut Portuguese
sausage into 1 inch chunks and brown in a
separate pan. Remove pork from broth and allow
to cool. Cut into 1 ½ to 2 inch chunks.

Add garbanzo beans, onions, ulu and kale to
broth. When vegetables are cooked add pork and
sausage chunks. Simmer for 20-30 minutes, add
macaroni during last 15 minutes. Add water as
needed during cooking.

(taro)
Pot Roast Chicken with Ulu
Adapted from a Chinese style chicken with taro dish

4 pound chicken (fryer or roaster)
2 cloves garlic
2 tablespoons oil
¾ cup water
½ cup dark thick shoyu
¼ cup wine
1 piece ginger
3 cups boiled mature ulu, cut into 2 inch pieces.

Rub dark shoyu and garlic on chicken and in cavity. Heat dutch oven and brown on all sides. Add sauce and simmer about 30 minutes. Add ulu pieces and finish cooking (about 30 more minutes).

Salmon Croquettes

3 to 4 cups cooked ulu, mashed
1/2 medium round onion, chopped
2 tablespoons chopped green onion
1 clove garlic
12 ounces (about 1½ cups) canned salmon with
    bones, drained (reserve liquid)
2 eggs
salt and pepper to taste
flour and panko (crispy white bread crumbs)
oil for frying

Mix all ingredients together except flour. Whip light and somewhat fluffy. Form 3 inch oblong patties (foot ball shapes), coat lightly with flour and panko (crispy bread crumbs). Deep fry until golden brown. Serve with hot sauce or shoyu.

Savory Chili Stuffed Ulu

1 mature Ulu, baked or boiled cut into thirds to make boats.

Chili:
2 pounds chuck roast, cut into 1 inch cubes
1 medium or 1 cup round onion, chopped
2 cloves garlic, minced
1 stalk celery, chopped
2 teaspoons salt
1 teaspoon cracked black pepper
2 tablespoons chili powder
1 teaspoon liquid pepper sauce
2 tablespoons chili powder
1 1/2 cups water

Remove core from Ulu and remove a ½ inch layer to enlarge cavity. Coarsely chop ulu and reserve.

In a large saucepan, brown beef well. Add onion, garlic and celery. Cook until tender. Add seasonings and water, simmering until tender. To thicken add chopped ulu. Fill each ulu boat with chili meat and serve.

(Potato)
Ulu and Ham Casserole
A variation of a classic ham and potato casserole

4 to 5 cups mature green ulu, chunks boiled
2 tablespoons oil
1 clove garlic
1 medium onion chopped
2 stalks celery chopped
1 cup frozen green peas
2 cups diced ham

White Sauce:
>4 tablespoons butter
>3 tablespoons flour
>2 cups dairy or soy milk
>½ teaspoon salt
>¼ teaspoon pepper

Heat butter and flour, cooking to form a paste (roux). Cook for 2-3 minutes until cooked but not brown. Slowly add milk, salt and pepper using a whisk, until smooth. Sauce will appear thin. Do not boil.

In large dutch oven, heat oil, add onions, garlic and celery and cook until clear. Add ulu and ham. Heat through and add white sauce. Pour into a 9 by 13 inch pan, sprayed with cooking spray. Cover with foil. Bake in a 350 degree oven for about 60 minutes. Remove cover during last 15 minutes to brown.

Optional: Top with toasted breadcrumbs, or potato chips before serving.

(potato)
Ulu Chicken Curry

6 chicken thighs
2 tablespoons olive oil
1 medium onion
2 cloves garlic chopped
2 medium carrots
2 stalks celery
2 cups mature cooked, green ulu chunks
½ teaspoon salt
½ teaspoon black pepper
2 tablespoons curry powder
1 cup soy or dairy milk

Cut chicken in 1 inch chunks, removing bones. Brown chicken meat and bones in olive oil. Cut remaining vegetables into large 1 to 2 inch chunks. Reduce heat and add onions, garlic and celery cooking until translucent. Add carrots and ulu. Add 2 cups water and simmer for 15 to 20 minutes until vegetables are tender. Remove Chicken bones and discard.

Remove 5 to 6 chunks of ulu and coarsely mash, set aside. Add salt pepper and curry to taste. Add milk and mashed ulu. Heat through gently. Mashed ulu will thicken the curry.

(Alternately, remove 1½ cups vegetables and broth. Blend in blender until smooth and return to pot).

(potato)
Ulu Codfish Patties

3 to 4 cups cooked ulu, mashed
1 medium round onion, chopped
1 clove garlic
1½ cups shredded codfish
2 eggs
3 tablespoons chopped Chinese Parsley
1 teaspoon fresh oregano (or ½ teaspoon dried)
salt and pepper to taste
flour
oil for frying

Soak codfish in water until excess salt is removed. Drain codfish and mix with remaining ingredients except flour. Form 2 to 3 inch patties, coat lightly with flour. Heat 2 to 3 tablespoons oil in a pan. Fry until golden brown. Serve with hot sauce or shoyu.

* To make Croquettes: mash ulu and whip until fluffy, adding ½ to ¾ cup dairy or soy mild. Mix in remaining ingredients except flour. Form into 3 inch oblongs, dust lightly with flour and deep fry until golden brown.

(potato)
Ulu Corned Beef Hash Patties
This is a variation of corned beef hash with potatoes

3 to 4 cups cooked ulu, mashed
1 medium round onion, chopped
1 clove garlic
2 stalks celery, chopped (optional)
1 can corned beef or (1¼ cups shredded fresh,
    cooked corned beef)
2 eggs
salt and pepper to taste
2 tablespoons Italian flat parsley or green onion,
chopped (optional)
flour
oil for frying

Mix ingredients except flour and oil. Form 2 to 3 inch patties, coat lightly with flour. Heat 2 to 3 tablespoons oil. Fry until golden brown. Serve with hot sauce or ketchup.

(potato)
Ulu Crusted Fish

1½ pounds fresh fish fillet (Ono or Mahimahi)
4 tablespoons garlic chili sauce

Mix together:
4 to 5 cups mature green ulu, mashed
2 teaspoons salt
¼ teaspoon pepper
4 tablespoons butter
2 cloves crushed garlic
Fresh basil or Cilantro leaves for garnish

Cut fish into 3 to 4 ounces pieces (about the size of a deck of playing cards). Marinade for 5 to 10 minutes. Coat a baking dish with cooking spray. Place about 3 tablespoons of mashed ulu in a mound on a baking dish. Place a piece of fish on top of mashed ulu. Cover fish with a layer of ulu and cover sides of fish. Repeat until all the fish covered. Brush with melted butter or olive oil. Bake in a 375 degree oven for 25 to 30 minutes until Ulu is light brown and fish is cooked.

Alternate Fish Seasonings:
Cracked pepper and crushed garlic
Curry powder and grated ginger;
Hoi Sin Sauce and Oyster Sauce
Fresh dill

(potato)
Ulu Frittata

2 tablespoons olive oil
1 medium onion cut to ½ inch pieces
½ teaspoon Shoyu
1 ½ cups mature ulu boiled and sliced
1 large canned pimento, chopped (or roast a red
    bell pepper and chop)
12 eggs slightly beaten
¼ cup mozzarella cheese, cubed (or 4 slices
    Veggie slices tm)
1 tablespoon chopped Italian parsley or thyme

 Add olive oil to a large, heated cast iron pan (10-12 inches). Add onion to oil cooking until onion is transparent. Add about ½ teaspoon shoyu and cook until brown. Add sweet boiled ulu and pimento. Sprinkle cheese over top of ulu mixture and immediately pour eggs over vegetables. Cook for 2-3 minutes until the bottom of eggs are firm. Place entire pan under broiler (about 4 inches away) and broil for 3-5 minutes until top is fluffy and firm but not dry. To serve, run a spatula around edge of pan and invert onto a large plate and cut in to wedges.

(green banana)
Ulu Pastelles
Puerto Rican Pork Classic

Meat filling:
5 pounds pork, cut into ¾ inch cubes
½ cup achote oil (or use achote powder)
10 cloves garlic crushed
3 tablespoons fresh chopped oregano
6 ounces canned tomato paste
3 round onions chopped
3 cups chopped cilantro
4 ½ ounce can chopped olives
1 Hawaiian chili pepper
1 tablespoon salt
2 teaspoons black pepper
3 cans pitted black olives (set aside)

Brown pork in achote oil. Add garlic and onions and saute' until onions are translucent. Add remaining ingredients except whole olives. Simmer for about 30 minutes. Allow mixture to cool

Ulu Mixture: Masa
3 green mature ulu, peeled and cored
3 green mature ulu, mashed
Salt to taste
2-3 cups achote oil/and or achote powder
(enough to make it orange-red)

Finely grate ulu (finest blade on food processor or Champion juicer). Mix 1 part raw shredded ulu with one part cooked, mashed ulu, salt and achote oil until masa is a yellow-orange color. Mix well and set aside.

Achote oil:
4 cups oil
2 cups achote seed

Heat oil with achote seed on low heat for 15 to 20 minutes. Do not fry seeds or they will burn, turning the oil bitter. Set aside and strain oil. Store left over oil in refrigerator.

Banana Leaf Preparation. Pick large banana leaves. Remove ribs from leaves and wash. Burn each leaf until shiny over gas stove to soften. Cut into pieces to line foil wraps.

To assemble Pastelles:
On a 12 inch square of aluminum foil, place a piece of softened banana leaf (about 4X8 inches). Put a tablespoon of achote oil on the banana leaf. Place about ½ cup of the masa on the oil. Spread it with the back of a spoon. Place 2 rounded tablespoons of filling in the middle of the masa. Place 2 olives in center of filling. Match and roll down the center of the foil then roll up the ends, sealing well. Each packet should be oblong, about the same size to allow for even cooking time.

Steam or boil for 1½ hour.

Pastelles freeze well either cooked or uncooked. Pastelles can be cooked straight from the freezer, allowing for additional cooking time.

* Achote is also called Annatto.

(green banana)
Ulu Pot Pastelles
"Pastelles De Olla"
A home style version of a Puerto Rican Classic

Filling:
3 pounds pork cut into ¾ inch cubes
½ cup achote oil (or use achote powder)
6 cloves garlic crushed
2 tablespoons fresh chopped oregano
8 ounces canned tomato sauce
2 medium onions chopped
2 cups chopped cilantro
1 small can chopped olives, about 4½ ounces
1 Hawaiian chili pepper
1 tablespoon salt
2 teaspoons black pepper
2 cans small pitted black olives (set aside)
1 large or 2 medium sized mature, green ulu,
    peeled, cored and finely grated
2 cups water

In a covered pot, brown pork in achote oil. (See recipe on page 82). Add garlic and onions and sauté' until onions are translucent. Add remaining ingredients except whole olives. Cook on low heat about 90 minutes. Place a large piece of soften banana leaf on top of the pot inside the lid. (This will give the pastelles its traditional flavor!) Remove the banana leaf when you stir the mixture and replace it on top while cooking. Stir often. Add more water or chicken stock if needed. Add whole olives just before serving.

Ulu Pot Pie

3 cups mature green ulu cut into 1 inch pieces
2 chicken breasts, deboned, cut into 1 inch cubes
2 tablespoons vegetable oil
1 clove garlic crushed
1 medium onion
1 stalk celery, chopped (optional)
1 medium carrot
½ cup frozen green peas
½ cup water
½ teaspoon salt
½ teaspoon pepper
1 cup milk (soy or dairy)

Boil ulu until tender and drain. Remove ½ cup, mash and set aside. Brown chicken in oil with garlic. Cut vegetables into 1 inch pieces. Add onions, celery and carrots and water cooking until tender. Add green peas and milk. To thicken, add mashed ulu. Mixture will thicken as it cooks.

Single Crust: 1½ cups flour
                  ½ teaspoon salt
                  ½ cup + 1 Tablespoon shortening
                  3 scant Tablespoons ice water

Pour stew into 9 inch deep pie pan and cover with pastry crust. Slash top of crust to vent. Bake in a 400 degree oven for 30 to 45 minutes until crust is golden brown. For double crust, (double crust recipe) bake for 15 minutes at 400 degrees then lower heat to 350 degrees for about 45 minutes, baking until crust is a light brown and juices begin to bubble.

(potato)
Ulu Shepard's Pie

1 medium mature green ulu, boiled
1 block or ½ cup butter
½ teaspoon salt
½ teaspoon pepper

1½ pounds ground beef
2 cloves garlic, crushed
1 medium onion, chopped
1 stalk celery, chopped (optional)
2 -16 ounce bag frozen mixed vegetables
2 cups water
1 teaspoon salt
½ teaspoon pepper

Peel, core and dice ulu. Boil until tender and drain. Mash while warm with butter, salt and pepper and set aside.

Brown ground beef and drain oil. Add garlic, onions and celery and cook until translucent. Add frozen mixed vegetables, water and seasoning. Divide into 2 large loaf pans. Cover with mashed ulu. Bake in a 350 degree oven covered for 30 minutes. Remove cover and bake for about 15 more minutes until top is brown. Let sit for a few minutes before serving.

Ulu Spinach Lasagna
This recipe uses sliced ulu in place of traditional noodles

1 large ulu
1 recipe meat sauce or use bottled sauce
1 pound ricotta cheese
1 pound shredded mozzarella cheese
1 pound frozen spinach, thawed and squeezed
Parmesan cheese curls for garnish

To prepare Ulu "Lasagna Noodles", peel and quarter a large ulu. Boil a ulu until it is easily pierced with a fork but is still firm. Cut into 1/8 to ¼ inch slices and set aside.

Assemble lasagna in an extra deep pan. Spray pan with cooking spray. Spread a layer of sauce on the bottom of the pan. Carefully place sliced ulu in a layer lining the bottom of the pan. Spoon another layer of sauce to cover.

Spread a layer of spinach and cover with a layer of ulu slices. Place ricotta cheese and half the mozzarella on the ulu. Cover with another layer of sauce. Top with a third layer of ulu and cover with sauce and sprinkle with mozzarella cheese. Reserve Parmesan cheese to make curls to serve on top of each serving.

Bake at 350 degrees covered for 40-50 minutes until it bubbles. Let stand for 15 minutes before cutting and serving.

Ulu Lasagna – continued

Spicy Meat Sauce:

Cook together, drain excess oil
- ¼ cup olive oil
- 4 large cloves garlic, crushed
- 1 pound ground beef
- 1 pound ground pork

Add:
- 1 large yellow onion chopped
- 2 stalks celery chopped
- 1 large carrot, grated (optional)
- 1 cup water or stock
- ½ teaspoon salt
- ½ teaspoon ground black pepper
- ½ teaspoon red pepper flakes (optional)
- 2 - 28 oz. cans tomatoes (diced or pureed)
- 1 12 ounce can tomato paste
- 1 12 ounce can sliced mushrooms or 8 ounces
  fresh sliced mushrooms

Mix together and reserve half of herbs
- ½ cup chopped fresh basil
- ¼ cup chopped fresh Italian flat parsley
- 1 tablespoon chopped fresh oregano
- 1 tablespoon chopped fresh rosemary

Simmer half of herbs and all ingredients for about an hour, stirring occasionally. Stir in remaining half of herbs at end of cooking time.

Ulu Stuffed with Pork Hash

1 firm green or half ripe ulu (about 6-8 inches), cut in half and cored

Pork hash filling:
11/2 pounds ground pork
1/2 pound Chinese fish cake
1 can water chestnut, drained and chopped
1 ball Chinese salted turnip (chung choi) rinsed
    and chopped
2 eggs beaten
1 teaspoon soy sauce
1 teaspoon sugar
2 tablespoons oyster sauce (optional)
¼ cup green onions, chopped

Wash and core ulu. Mix all filling ingredients well. Cut ulu in half and scoop out center, leaving a 1-1/2 inch shell. Fill each ulu half, mounding pork hash. Place in 9X13 inch baking pan with 1 cup water at bottom of pan. Cover pan with foil and bake at 350 degrees for 60 minutes. Remove foil after 60 minutes and bake uncovered for 20-30 minutes until top is brown. Ulu is done when it is fork or chopstick "tender" and pork hash is thoroughly cooked. Let ulu rest for 10 to 15 minutes before serving.

Alternately, cut about 1/3 of the top of the ulu, remove core and scoop out the core and some of the ulu to make a bowl. Fill as above, making a mound on top of the ulu, bake as above increasing cooking time by about 30 minutes.

Ulu Tuna Patties

3-4 cups cooked ulu, mashed
1/2 medium round onion, chopped
1 stalk celery chopped
2 cans (6 ounces each) tuna, drained
2 eggs
salt and pepper to taste
flour
oil for frying

Mix all ingredients together except flour. Form 3-4 inch patties, coat lightly with flour. Fry until golden brown. Serve with hot sauce or shoyu.

Ulu with Pigeon Peas
Gandule "Rice" Style Ulu

4 cups chopped mature ulu
¾ pound pork or chicken sliced
5 cups water
1 ½ cups Pigeon peas (1 cup fresh or 1
    12 ounce can)
2 cloves garlic
1 tablespoon fresh chopped oregano leaves
2 tsp salt
½ teaspoon pepper
½ cup achote oil (may reduce oil and substitute
annatto powder to taste)
1 medium onion chopped
¾ cup Chinese parsley, (cilantro) chopped

Pare and core firm, mature ulu. Chop coarsely in
food processor until it is about the size of large
grains of rice.

In a large heavy bottom pan, brown pork (or
chicken) in a bit of achote oil. Cook with garlic,
and oregano. salt and pepper. Add water and
peas to meat. When meat is tender, add
remaining Achote oil, onion and Chinese parsley.
Cook over medium heat for 15 minutes. Add ulu
and simmer for 15 to 20 minutes until ulu is tender
but still holds its shape. Add salt and pepper
stirring gently and serve.

(potato)
Vegetable Ulu Curry

1 pound seitan or 1 block firm tofu, cut in to 1 inch
    pieces
2 tablespoon olive oil
3-4 cloves garlic chopped
1 medium onion
2 medium carrots
2 stalks celery
2 cups mature cooked, ulu chunks
½ teaspoon salt
½ teaspoon black pepper
2 tablespoons curry powder
1 cup soy or dairy milk

Cut chicken in 1 inch chunks, removing bones.
Brown seitan or tofu in garlic and olive oil.
Remove from pot and set aside. Cut remaining
vegetables into large 1-2 inch chunks.

Reduce heat and add onions and celery cooking
until translucent. Add carrots and ulu. Add 2 cups
water and simmer for 15 to 20 minutes until
vegetables are tender. Return browned tofu or
seitan to pot. Remove 5 to 6 chunks of ulu and
coarsely mash, set aside. Add salt pepper and
curry to taste. Add milk and mashed ulu. Heat
through gently. Mashed ulu will thicken the curry.

(Alternately, remove 1½ cups vegetables and
broth. Blend in blender until smooth and return to
pot).

Vegetarian Ulu Lasagne
This recipe uses sliced ulu in place of traditional noodles.

1 large mature, green ulu
1 recipe marinara sauce or use your favorite
    bottled sauce
11/2 pounds tofu, mashed and drained
½ pound soy or rice "pepper" cheese
½ pound frozen spinach, thawed and squeezed
2 large yellow squash, steamed or par boiled,
    sliced
2 large zucchini steamed or par boiled, sliced
1 12 ounce can red pimento or 2 large red bell
    peppers roasted and peeled

To prepare ulu "Lasagne Noodles", peel and
quarter a large ulu. Boil ulu until it is easily
pierced with a fork but is still firm. Cut into 1/8
inch slices and set aside.

Assemble lasagne in an extra deep pan. Spread a
layer of sauce on the bottom of the pan. Carefully
place sliced ulu in a layer lining the bottom of the
pan. Spoon another layer of sauce to cover.
Spread tofu in a thin layer and cover with sauce.
Top with a layer of ulu and sauce. Repeat
layering placing spinach with yellow squash in
one layer then zucchini with red pimento in the
next, ending with ulu and more sauce.

Bake at 350 degrees covered for 40-50 minutes
until it bubbles. Let stand for 15 minutes before
cutting and serving.

Top each serving with a slice of pepper jack soy
cheese.

Vegetarian Lasagne – *continued*

Spicy Marinara Sauce

Cook together,
    ¼ cup olive oil
    3-4 large cloves garlic, crushed
    1 cup chopped seitan or 1 cup textured
        vegetable protein
Add:
2 large yellow onion chopped
2 stalks celery chopped
1 large carrot, grated (optional)
2 cups water
½ teaspoon salt
½ teaspoon ground black pepper
½ teaspoon red pepper flakes (optional)
2 - 28 oz. cans tomatoes (diced or pureed)
1 -12 ounce can tomato paste
1- 12 ounce can sliced mushrooms or 8 ounces
   fresh sliced mushrooms

Mix together and reserve half of herbs
    ½ cup chopped fresh basil
    ¼ cup chopped fresh Italian flat parsley
    1 tablespoon chopped fresh oregano
    1 tablespoon chopped fresh rosemary

Simmer half of herbs and all ingredients for about an hour, stirring occasionally. Stir in remaining half of herbs at end of cooking time.

Alternative… Substitute you favorite white sauce (made with soy milk) in the spinach layer for something really special…

Vegetarian Ulu Nishime
Japanese Vegetable Stew

1 large gobo (burdock root) peeled, (soak in water
    until ready to be cooked)
1 12 ounce can takenoko (bamboo shoots)
1 large piece hasu,l otus root, peeled (2 cups)
12 shiitake, dried mushroom, soak in water,
    remove stem and cut in half
12 black cloud fungus, soaked and cleaned
1 12 ounce can button mushrooms
2 medium carrots, peeled
1 8 ounce can water chestnuts
1 large piece Nishime konbu, seaweed, soaked
 2 cups mature, green ulu
4 pieces Konnaku (yam cake) cut into pointed
    pieces
1 medium daikon (white radish) optional
1 package Aburage, cut into ½ inch slices
4 cups water
3 pieces ginger (2 inches by ½ inch thick)
3 tablespoons salt
3 tablespoons sugar or 9 packages Splenda tm

Cut vegetables into 1 inch chunks. Set aside
soaked in water to keep fresh. Soak and wash
konbu. Cut into 2 inch wide strips and tie into
knots at 3 inch intervals. Cut pieces midway
between each knot. Set aside.

Bring water to a boil with ginger salt and sugar.
Add shiitake mushroom, button mushroom and
black fungus. Simmer for 15-20 minutes to flavor
broth. Add takenoko, hasu, water chestnuts,
konnaku, aburage and nishime konbu. Simmer

Vegetarian Ulu Nishime - *continued*

until konbu is almost tender. Add ulu, carrots and gobo (daikon optional). Simmer until vegetables are tender. Rounding edges of the ulu pieces makes it appear more like Japanese taro.

Alternative: Crack a raw egg on very hot rice and top with a generous serving of Stew. Cover bowl immediately and let sit for a few minutes to allow the egg to cook.

This is a vegetarian version of Umani (with chicken) or Nishime when cooked with pork or beef.

Vegetarian Ulu Pastelles
Puerto Rican Tamale

Filling:
6 cups seitan or firm tofu, cut into ½ inch cubes
½ cup achote oil (or use achiote powder)
10 cloves garlic crushed
3 tablespoons fresh chopped oregano
1 small can tomato paste
3 round onions chopped
3 cups chopped cilantro
1 small can chopped olives
1 Hawaiian chili pepper
1 tablespoon salt
2 teaspoons black pepper
3 cans pitted black olives (set aside)

Brown Seitan or Tofu in achote oil. (seitan or tofu can also be quickly deep fried and drained for chewier texture). Add garlic and onions and sauté until onions are translucent. Add remaining ingredients except whole olives. Simmer for about 30 minutes. Allow mixture to cool.

Ulu Mixture: Masa
3 green mature ulu, peeled and cored
3 green cooked mashed ulu.
Salt to taste
2-3 cups achote oil/and or achote powder
(enough to make it orange-red)

See page 82, Ulu Pastelles for assembly instructions.

Chapter 7

Desserts
Ripe Ulu

 The ulu is Ripe when the skin beings to turn from a yellow green to brown. Sap will not ooze from the stem when it is picked. It will soften and "sit down" on it self. A mature ulu will ripen and soften in 2 to 3 days. The aroma becomes sweet and the core can usually be removed by pulling the stem. This creates the cavity to stuff the sweet ulu.

The ripe ulu cooks quickly and is very soft and sticky. A very ripe ulu is mushy. The cooked pulp works well in place of pumpkin and the raw pulp can replace mashed banana in breads.

Boiled or Steamed Ulu

Steam, bake or microwave the ripe ulu whole, first pulling out the stem. For faster cooking, cut in half and place a pat of butter in each cavity and steam cut side down in a covered pan.

Baked Ulu Mochi with Coconut
A variation of a Filipino favorite using sweet potato

Mix together:
1 pound mochiko (rice flour), sifted
2 teaspoons baking powder
¾ cup sugar

Mix together and add to mochiko and sugar
mixture above:
1 ½ cups milk (dairy or soy)
1 ½ cups coconut milk
1 12 ounce bottle macapuno coconut strings
    (drained)
3 eggs
1½ cups mashed ripe ulu

Lightly sift mochiko powder. Mix dry ingredients together. Add liquid ingredients and eggs to make a smooth batter. Add mashed ulu and drained coconut. Pour into a greased 9 by 13 inch pan. Bake at 350 degrees for about 1½ hours. Cut with a plastic knife when cool.

(sweet potato)

Crispy Sweet Ulu Balls

1 cup mashed sweet ulu
¼ cup sugar
3/4 cup rice flour (mochiko)
3/4 cup water

Mix ingredients together until smooth. Drop by rounded teaspoons full into hot oil until dark brown. Drain on absorbent paper. Dust with powdered sugar and serve.

(purple yam)

Halo Halo with Sweet Ulu
Oriental style ice dessert

2 cups half ripe ulu + ½ cup sugar
    or 2 cups ripe ulu
Coconut strips (Macapuno strings)
Sweet red beans, bottled
Coco palm sugar bottled
Evaporated milk or soy milk.
Shaved Ice

Boil ulu until tender. Drain except for ¼ cup water. Add sugar if using half ripe ulu and continue cooking for 15 minutes.

Fill a cup or bowl half way with finely shaved or cracked ice. Top with ulu, coconut strips, red beans, coco palm as desired. Top with milk. Serve.

(red beans)
Layered Ulu Manju
A variation on a classic Oriental Red Bean paste Dessert.
Sweet ripe ulu replaces tsubushi-an

Dough:

>5 cups flour
>½ cup sugar
>½ tsp salt
>1 lb or 2 cups butter
>¾ c milk, dairy or soy milk
>1 egg

Filling:

>3 cups mashed sweet ripe ulu
>¼ cup sugar optional)

Cream butter. Add alternately dry ingredients and milk in 3 portions. Divide dough in half.

Spread half of the dough in a 9 by 13 inch pan. Bake bottom for 10 minutes in a 375 degree oven. Remove pan from oven. . Spread mashed ulu on baked dough. Cover ulu with remaining dough. Brush egg over top of dough. Bake in a 375 degree oven for 35 to 40 minutes.

Serving suggestion: cut in squares and place in muffin cups to serve.

(acorn squash)
Stuffed Sweet Ulu
This is a great side dish....like stuffed acorn squash

1 mature ripe ulu
Filling – Mix together
    ¾ cup dried apricots, chopped
    2 tablespoons golden raisins
    2 tablespoons dried cranberries
    2 tablespoon macadamia nut pieces
    2 tablespoon brown sugar
    2 tablespoons butter

Wash and core ripe ulu, pulling out stem. Trim off about 1 inch of the top edge of the ulu. Fill ulu with fruit and nut mixture, Wrap in foil, place in a shallow pan and bake in a 350 degree oven for about 60 minutes.

Sweet Ulu Undagi
Okinawan drop doughnuts

1½ cups sugar
3 eggs
½ cup milk (may substitute water or soy milk)
1½ cups cooked sweet ripe ulu, chopped
3 cups flour
1 Tablespoon baking powder

Beat together sugar and eggs. Mix together ½ cup milk with mashed sweet ulu. Sift together 3 cups flour and 1 tablespoon baking powder. Add egg and sugar mixture to ulu mixture until well blended. Add flour mixture. Do not over mix.

Drop by spoonfuls and deep fry until golden brown.

(black bean)
Ulu Chien Doi
Adapted from a traditional Chinese Dim Sum Dessert

1 ½ cups brown sugar
1 ¼ cups hot water
3 ¾ cups (1 pound) mochi flour
Sesame seeds
Oil for frying

Filling: Mix ulu pulp with sugar and set aside
½ ripe baked or steamed breadfruit
½ cups sugar

Dissolve brown sugar in hot water. Set aside to cool. Stir liquid into flour making stiff dough. Shape into a 1½ inch diameter roll. Cut into ½ inch slices and flatten. Place about a tablespoon of sweet ulu filling in each slice of dough. Pinch edges of dough together to seal and roll into a ball. Roll in sesame seeds.

Deep fry balls in oil until golden brown. Press balls against side of pan while cooking so balls will expand.

Sweet Ulu Crunch
Adapted from a classic pumpkin dessert

Layer 1 - Crust: Mix together and spread in
      the bottom of a 9 by 13 inch pan

      1½ cups white cake mix
      2 Tablespoons brown sugar
      ¼ cup melted butter
      1 egg

Layer 2: Mix together then pour over crust.

      4 cups mashed ripe cooked breadfruit
      3 eggs
      1 teaspoon cinnamon
      ¼ teaspoon fresh grated nutmeg
      ¼ cup brown sugar
      1 cup milk (dairy or soy)

Layer 3: Sprinkle over first two layers. Bake for
      45 to 50 minutes at 350 degrees.

      1 box white cake mix minus 1 ½ cups mix
      2 tablespoons brown sugar
      ¼ c butter, melted (drizzle over top)
      ½ teaspoon cinnamon sprinkled
      Grating fresh nutmeg

Cake is done when toothpick comes clean from center of cake. Let cake cool in pan. Serve with whipped cream or nondairy topping sprinkled with salted macadamia nuts

Sweet Ulu Fritters

Mix:
1½ cups sugar
3 eggs
¾ cup milk (or soy milk)

Sift:
3 cups flour
1 Tablespoon baking powder

3/8 inch thick cooked ripe or half ripe ulu slices

Beat together sugar and eggs. Add milk. Sift together 3 cups flour and 1 tablespoon baking powder. Add egg and sugar mixture to flour mixture. Do not over mix.

Dip ulu in to batter one slice at a time and deep fry until golden brown.

Sweet Ulu Ice Cream

1 cup soft ripe ulu cooked and mashed
½ cup sugar
2 cups light cream or soymilk
2 eggs, slightly beaten
¼ teaspoon nutmeg optional

Pull out stem from ripe breadfruit. Bake or steam. Scoop out pulp. Mix with sugar, eggs and milk. Cook over low heat, stirring constantly. Remove from heat when custard starts to thicken. Continue stirring. Refrigerate custard until very cold. Pour into Ice Cream maker and freeze according to manufacture's directions.

Alternately, place chilled custard in the freezer in a flat tray and stir every 15 to 20 minutes until frozen.

Sweet Ulu Lavosh

3 cups flour
½ teaspoon baking soda
½ teaspoon salt
3 tablespoons sugar

Cut in:
          ½ cup butter (1 block)
Mix in:
          1 cup buttermilk (1 tablespoon vinegar
             plus enough milk to make 1 cup)
          1 cup mashed sweet ripe ulu
          6 tablespoons sesame seed

Add milk and mashed ulu mixture to dry ingredients. Dough will be slightly sticky. Form dough into 8-10 small balls. Coat each ball with sesame seeds. Roll dough out thin on a floured board. Bake on an ungreased cookie sheet for 10-15 minutes in a 400 degree preheated oven.

Cool on a wire rack until crisp. Return to oven for 5-10 minutes if crackers are not crispy once cooled. Store in an airtight container.

(Optional) sprinkle top lightly with sugar before baking.

Serve with softened sweet (unsalted) butter or honey butter.

(banana)

Sweet Ulu Lumpia

Adapted from a classic Filipino dessert made with bananas

1 whole ripe soft Ulu, steamed or boiled.
½ cup brown sugar
½ teaspoon cinnamon, optional
Lumpia wrappers
Oil for deep frying

Steam a soft, ripe ulu until firm. Scoop out pulp and mash with sugar and cinnamon. Wrap ulu in the lumpia wrapper, sealing with a light spray of water. Fry until golden brown.

(banana)

Sweet Ulu Macadamia Nut Bread

2 cups flour
2 teaspoon baking soda
1 teaspoon cinnamon
½ teaspoon salt
1 cup vegetable oil
1 teaspoon vanilla
1 ¼ cups sugar
3 eggs
1 cup cooked ripe ulu, mashed
¼ cup coarsely chopped macadamia nuts
1 cup golden raisins (optional)

Combine dry ingredients in a large bowl (sift baking soda if lumpy). Make a well and add remaining ingredients and mix. Pour into 2, greased and floured loaf pans. Bake at 325 degrees until done (about 50-60 minutes).

(azuki or lima beans)

Sweet Ulu Manju
Adapted from a traditional Japanese dessert

Dough:
> 5 cups flour
> 1 teaspoon salt
> 2 cups vegetable oil
> ¾ cup water

Filling:
> 3 cups mashed sweet ulu
> ½ cup sugar (optional, to taste)

Shape dough into walnut sized balls. Flatten on the palm of hand and place about 1 tablespoon filling in the center. Seal dough by pinching edges together. Brush tops with milk. Bake on an ungreased cookie sheet in a 400 degree oven for 25 minutes.

Alternative: Traditional butter pastry
2 sticks butter
1 stick or ½ cup margarine
3 cups flour
1 tablespoons sugar
¼ cup iced water or milk (dairy or soy)

Cut butter and margarine in flour and sugar. Sprinkle top with water and mix until moistened and just holds together (like pie crust). Shape as above.

Sweet Ulu Mochi

Ulu Story: My aunty gave me this "recipe" … saying there was no recipe.. Just mix some mochi ko (rice flour) with water until it was like a thick pancake batter, add sugar if you want and mix in the ulu about "this much", showing me a cupped hand, about ½ cup to start.

½ cup sweet, cooked mashed ulu
½ cup glutinous rice flour (mochiko)
2 to 3 tablespoons sugar
1 cup water

Mix all ingredients together. Should be the consistency of thick pancake batter. Drop by spoonfuls into hot oil. Remove when golden brown. Drain on absorbent paper.

(azuki beans)

Sweet Ulu Mochi with Kinako
Mochi:
1 ½ cups cooked sweet ulu, mashed
1 cup sugar
1 box (16 oz.) mochiko
1 cup water

½ cup kinako mix (roasted soy bean flour)

Mix mochi ingredients well. Shape into 1 inch balls. Drop into boiling water about 6 to 8 minutes. Balls will rise to the top when done. Drain on paper towels. Roll in kinako (1/4 cup kinako, ¼ cup sugar, 1/8 teaspoon salt). Makes about 5 dozens.

Sweet Ulu with Honey Won Tons

Filling:
>1 ripe ulu, cooked
>4 tablespoons honey
>Won ton wrappers
>Oil for frying
>Powdered (confectioners) sugar

Scoop about 2 cups pulp from a ripe ulu. Mash and mix with honey. Fill Won Ton wrappers with about 2 teaspoons of filling and fold slightly off the diagonal wetting edges with water to seal. Fry in medium heat oil until light brown. Drain on absorptive paper and sprinkle with confectioners sugar when cool. (If you want a sweeter dessert, sprinkle while slightly warm and more sugar will stick!)

Alternative: Make filling with about 1 tablespoon of honey. Drizzle honey on warm won tons and serve and 2 or 3 on a plate as an individual dessert. Great on top of vanilla ice cream.

Ulu "Sweet Potato" Pie
Adapted from a Southern classic

3 cups, soft ripe ulu cooked and mashed
½ cup sugar
1 cup milk, dairy or soy
2 teaspoons vanilla
2 eggs, slightly beaten
¼ teaspoon salt
¼ teaspoon nutmeg optional

Pull out stem from ripe breadfruit. Bake or steam. Scoop out pulp. Mix with sugar, milk, eggs, vanilla and remaining ingredients until smooth. Scrape into a deep 9 inch pie crust. (See page 112 for crust recipe). Bake for 15 minutes at 425 degrees then continue baking at 350 degrees for 45 minutes until set (knife inserted into center is wet but clean).

(dried fruit)
Ulu Coffee Cake

Batter: Mix together, adding ulu last
    1¼ cup flour
    3 tablespoons sugar
    1½ teaspoons baking powder
    ½ teaspoon salt
    2 tablespoons butter, softened
    ½ cup milk (dairy or soy)
    1 egg
    2/3 cup sweet ulu, cooked and chopped

Streusel: Mix together, cut in butter until crumbly
    ½ cup chopped nuts
    2 rounded tablespoon brown sugar
    ¼ cup flour
    ½ teaspoon cinnamon
    1/8 teaspoon fresh nutmeg
    3 tablespoons cold butter

Spread batter in an 8 by 8 inch square or 9 inch round baking pan coated with cooking spray. Sprinkle with Streusel. Bake in a 350 degree oven for 25 to 30 minutes. Toothpick inserted in center comes out clean when done.

Ulu Custard Pie

1½ cups, soft ripe raw ulu
½ cup sugar to taste
3 cups milk (dairy or soy)
4 eggs, beaten
2 teaspoons vanilla
¼ teaspoon salt
Grated fresh grated nutmeg (optional)

Mix ingredients together until smooth. Pour into a deep 9 inch pie crust. Bake at 425 degrees for 15 minutes, reduce temperature to 350 degrees for 45 minutes. Custard is done when edges are firm and center is slightly soft but not wet.

Single Crust: 1½ cups flour
                ½ teaspoon salt
                ½ cup + 1 Tablespoon shortening
                3 scant Tablespoons ice water

Cut flour and salt into shortening until crumbs are the size of peas. Sprinkle iced water onto flour mixture and work water into dough using fingers. Press dough together to make a ball. Flour dough and flatten it into a disk; smooth edges.

Roll dough between 2 sheets of waxed paper.

Remove top layer of waxed paper. Place a pie pan up side down on the pastry. Turn pastry over into pie pan, easing crust into pan. Remove waxed paper. Trim crust 1 inch larger than pan and fold edge under itself. If dough cracks, moisten edges with water and press together.

(azuki beans)
Ulu Dorayaki
Sweet Ulu Filled Pancakes

Batter:
- 2 cups flour
- 1½ teaspoons baking powder
- 2 teaspoons baking soda
- 1 teaspoon salt
- 2 Tablespoon sugar
- 2 eggs
- 1 cup dairy or soy milk plus 1 tablespoon vinegar (or buttermilk)
- 2 Tablespoons oil

Filling
- 1 ½ cups chopped cooked ripe ulu
- ½ cup sugar

Mix dry ingredients, sifting baking powder, baking soda and salt. Add egg mixture and oil to make a batter. Let batter rest for 5 minutes before cooking. Drop onto a medium hot griddle, turning when top is covered with bubbles.

Form walnut sized balls of ulu filling and flatten slightly. Place between 2 pancakes while warm to make dorayaki. Return to grill to warm through on each side.

* Griddle is hot enough when a tiny droplet of water dances on surface. If drop sits and bubbles in a few seconds, griddle is too cold.

Ulu Ice Cake
A great summer refresher

2 cups, soft ripe cooked ulu, mashed
½ cup sugar to taste
2 cups milk (dairy or soy)
1 cup water
2 teaspoons vanilla
1 bottle coconut strips (from oriental food aisle)

Mash ulu coarsely. Mix ingredients together. Pour into paper cups and freeze.

(azuki beans)
Ulu Yokan

½ cup or 1 stick kanten (argar)
1 cup water
3/4 cup sugar (or ½ cup sugar and 8 packets
    Splenda tm)
2 cups cooked sweet ulu

Break kantan into 1 inch pieces and soak kanten in water. Cook over low heat until kanten is dissolved. Add ulu and sugar. Cook over medium heat, stirring constantly until thick and fudge like. Pour into loaf pan and chill. Cut into slices and serve.

(Optional) add ½ cup chopped macadamia nuts when mixture is thick. Pour into pan as above.

Notes....

Substitutions... If you do not have breadfruit, ulu, almost all of the recipes have a substitution listed in the parentheses, or in the title of the recipe. For example, immature ulu "artichoke" represents recipes that can be used with artichokes or for recipes with (potato) in the top left hand corner, potato can be used in place of ulu. So, this cookbook is also about **artichoke, taro, potato, rice, sweet potato, yam, pumpkin, chestnut, azuki bean and banana.**

Soy milk and Soy cheese can replace of dairy milk and cheese. Vitasoy tm and Edensoy tm soy milk work very well in place of milk. Lifetime tm makes a meltable cheese that grates well and Veggie Slices tm is sold as wrapped single slices.

Eggs add flavor, color, acts as a binder and when beaten helps foods rise. The following replaces 1 large whole egg: 2 egg whites; 1 tablespoons psyllium powder blended with 3 tablespoons of water (makes about ¼ cup); 1 teaspoons xanthan gum blended with 3 tablespoons of water; 1 tablespoon soy protein powder blended with 2 tablespoons water.

To make a reduced fat dressing, blend 1 teaspoon of xanthan gum in 1 cup of water and use in place of all or a portion of oil.

Sugar adds flavor, texture and color to foods. Replace ½ to ¾ of sugar with Splenda tm, a heat stable sugar substitute. 1 packet of Splenda tm has the sweetness equivalent of 2 teaspoons of sugar. 3 packets of Splenda tm is equal to 2 tablespoons of sugar.

Visit us at:
www.ulucookbook.com

ORDER FORM

I would like to order additional copies of

The *Breadfruit* Cookbook

Number of copies _____ x $17.95 = $ _____

Shipping and Handling (1st copy)   = $ 4.00

Each additional copy _____ X $2.00 = $ _____

Total Cost of Order $ _____

Please send check or money order to:

Handworks
P.O. Box 215
Kapaa, Hawaii 96746

Or visit us online at:
www.ulucookbook.com

Send book to:

Name: _____

Address: _____

City:_____ State_____ Zip code_____

Telephone: (   ) _____